Prese
Just Thi

M000214320

Presence-Awareness:

Just This and Nothing Else

Talks with 'Sailor' Bob Adamson

Edited by John Wheeler

NON-DUALITY PRESS

NON-DUALITY PRESS

6 Folkestone Road Salisbury SP2 8JP United Kingdom
www.non-dualitybooks.com

Transcription and initial editing by John Wheeler

ISBN 0-9547792-4-X

Contents

Preface

The dialogues contained in this book are a testimony to 'Sailor' Bob Adamson's wisdom and clarity in action. Bob's words always go straight to the heart of matter. They are an uncompromising and direct pointing to the fact of our own being. His words are filled with warmth, energy, clarity and humour. His teaching is the essential message of non-duality presented in the most direct and clear terms. Bob is a rare treasure. For years, he has been one of the best kept 'open secrets' in the world of contemporary spirituality. Following the publication of his first book *What's Wrong with Right Now, Unless You Think About It?*, a growing number of seekers have been drawn to 'Sailor' Bob Adamson and his message.

I am privileged to be able to help bring out this second book of dialogues. I would like to express my appreciation to Julian Noyce of Non-Duality Press for his support in coordinating the layout and final editing of the book.

You will not find a more profound pointing to your real nature than what is contained in these pages.

John Wheeler
Santa Cruz, California
August, 2004

1. The Fact of Your Own Being

Bob: If you are seeking truth, reality, God (or whatever you like to call it) then start with the only reality you are absolutely certain of. That is the fact of your own being. Under no circumstances can you say you are not. The fact of your own being is the only thing you are absolutely sure of. That expresses through the mind as the thought 'I am'. You know that you are, and you say 'I am'. But that thought 'I am' is not the reality. It is only a thought. What it is expressing is that sense of presence, that knowing that you are, that awareness of being present right now. That knowingness is expressing through the mind as the thought 'I am'.

We base what we talk about here upon what the ancient traditions tell us. For instance, in Hinduism, they say that God or reality is nondual, meaning that it is one-without-a-second. There is nothing other than that. In the Dzogchen scriptures of Buddhism (Dzogchen is the ultimate Buddhism), they say it is 'non-conceptual, self-shining, ever-fresh presence-awareness, just this and nothing else'. All the traditions somewhere along the line will tell you, when speaking about reality, that it is omnipresence, omnipotence and omniscience. Omnipresence means pure and total presence, or all-presence. Omniscience means pure and total knowing, or all-knowing. Omnipotence means pure and total power, or all-power. 'All' means that it doesn't leave room for me, you or anything else. It is all that. That is why we say that what you are seeking you already are.

The search itself becomes a problem from that point of view. The search implies that you are going to get something that you haven't already got. That implies that if you haven't already got it, you are thinking of some future time in which you will be able to get it. But it is omnipresence! It is only now-ness or presence. If you can grasp that and

— 9 —

understand that, you will see that any search for it is futile. You will not find something at some future time, because there is no future time. If you have a look at that, you can see it quite clearly. You have got memory, which is the past; and you have got anticipation or imagination, which is about the future. What memory have you got right now if you are not thinking about it?

Q: Without thinking about it, what is the first thing that comes to mind?

Bob: No. Have you got a memory if you are not thinking about it?

Q: Well, no, I don't.

Bob: Can you anticipate or imagine a future without thought? When you are thinking about the past, the actual thinking is happening now, presently; and when you are anticipating or imagining the future, the actual thinking is happening presently. So, you really haven't moved into the past, or you haven't moved into the future, though we think we have. We are so conditioned to go along with the fluctuations of the mind that we think we are in the past or in the future. But the actual thinking is all the time going on presently. This is the actuality. The actual livingness is going on in this moment. You can't live a moment ago. You can recall it, but if you recall it, it is recalled presently. It is no longer the past. It is a fresh recollection happening now. Or you can imagine the future, but you can't live in the future. Someone might say, 'I was in the past' or 'I was way ahead in the future'. But that is only in the mind, only in the thought, not in the actuality.

That is why we say that what you are seeking you already are. You can't be anything other than that, really.

2. What is the Cause of Our Problems?

Bob: What is the cause of our problems? When we have a look at our problems, they all start from the belief in that separate entity, the idea that we are separate, a person, an entity. That comes about when we are about two or two and a half years old, when we start to reason. A little child, prior to that, is just living from the natural state, which is the primal mind, the natural mind. For example, you can take a little child, put him in front of a mirror and daub his face with paint and different colours. He will not know it's himself! He'll see the face, but he hasn't realised that 'That is me' at that stage. There is awareness there. He is aware of the reflection in the mirror and what it looks like, but there is no self-awareness there at that stage. The self-awareness comes upon us at about two and a half years old, when we start to reason. When we look at the mind, you will see how that happens.

I use the word intelligence-energy, rather than 'God' or 'spiritual' or whatever because everybody has got a different belief, religion or concept about God. When they try to align this with their concepts it doesn't add up in all cases. It all depends on what their concept is. Intelligence-energy is what functions this universe. The stars in their orbit, the earth going around the sun, the tides coming in and out, the seasons coming and going—all of this implies that there is an intelligence. The movement of all those things implies energy. That intelligence-energy is the same intelligence-energy that is beating your heart right now, breathing you, growing your hair and your fingernails, replacing the cells in your body and digesting your food. It is doing all those things effortlessly. There is no 'me' saying, 'I have got to digest my food' or 'I have got to take the next breath' or 'I have got to make sure my heart expands and contracts'. It is all happening naturally. It is only at about two and a half years of age that the 'I' thought comes upon us.

Look at thought. You will see that thought is subtle word. Words are sound. Sound is a vibration. So, vibration is only a movement of energy also. Take this body. This body can be broken down into the elements; it is made up of the elements. Earth is the flesh and bone. Air, which we breathe, provides the chi or prana (energy). Fire is the heat in the body that is keeping it going. Water: the body is about eighty percent water. Space: there is plenty of space in between the cells and everywhere else in this body. So, the body is nothing but the elements. They, in turn, can be broken down into subatomic particles and into just that pure intelligence-energy. It is just the same as this chair. It is seemingly a solid piece of furniture. But it can be broken down into subatomic particles that are whirling around at a terrific speed. So, it can all be broken down into that one intelligence-energy.

Have a look at your thought, and see how it is functioning. It is always functioning in the inter-related opposites. It is either in the past, which is memory, or it is in the future, which is anticipation or imagination. Within that range, it is constantly functioning in the opposites, good/bad, pleasant/painful, happy/sad, loving/hating, positive/negative. These are all relative to that reference point, that image that we have about ourselves.

When the 'I' thought comes upon us then there arises the opposite to 'I', which is 'not I' or 'other than I'. If there is something that you think is not I, well, you feel separate from that. You say, 'That is not I or not me'. There is a sense of separation. With that sense of separation comes insecurity and vulnerability. From that time on, we are seeking to be secure and less vulnerable. That is really when the search starts. It is not a so-called 'spiritual search' at that stage. It is a search to acquire, to become whole, complete, secure and less vulnerable. We are conditioned to look 'out there'. To start off, the little child wants a warm, loving family around it. If it has got a warm loving family, it will feel much more secure and less vulnerable. Families form into tribes. In the old days they used to call them tribes. The bigger and stronger my tribe is, the more secure I'll be, and the less vulnerable. Today nations form into nations, and nations fight with nations because of that sense of insecurity and vulnerability.

3. You are Being Lived

Bob: The man with the book open, all ready to go!

Q: *In the book here, at one point there is a question: 'But the nature of thought affects the activity of the world'. You say, 'Exactly'. Then the questioner says, 'So, this means that your life and what happens depends on your awareness?' You say, 'Yes, in other words, you are being lived'.*

Bob: Yes?

Q: *I think my question comes from a mind that is still trying to understand. But thoughts seem to have an effect on our actions.*

Bob: Yes?

Q: *So thoughts, well, let's say there are ignorant thoughts. Let's say the thoughts are, 'I'm just going to fail and not get the job'. That has an effect on your confidence when you are sitting in the interview and you don't get the job.*

Bob: Yes?

Q: *Then those thoughts have affected that action.*

Bob: Yes. So, who thinks they are thinking that thought, 'I am just going to fail'? All your problems arise from that idea of a separate entity.

Q: *Yes.*

Bob: The energy just goes into that belief. It does affect it from that point of view, doesn't it?

Q: Thoughts arise from the belief in that self-centre?

Bob: No! Thoughts arise.

Q: Problems arise?

Bob: Yes, all problems are problems from the idea of a separate entity.

Q: So, are all successes problems?

Bob: If you think you have had a success! It all comes back to whether or not you believe yourself to be that separate entity. If you say 'I'm positive' or 'I'm successful', it is the same as if you are saying 'I'm failing' or 'I can't do it'.

Q: I think I'm obsessed with keeping myself, the sense of self, and turning it from negative to positive, rather than questioning the very sense of self.

Bob: Yes. But what can keep it, and what can turn it? You have got to understand: it is one-without-a-second. Basically, it is one-without-a-second, nondual. Now, from that point of view, is there anyone or anything that can turn it or alter it or modify it or correct it in any way? Even the thought itself must be that also.

Q: There seems to be something that can turn it.

Bob: (*Laughing*) You are just a dreamer trying to change the dream, from that point of view!

Q: Yes.

Bob: What value is that?

Q: But, hang on: at some point the cloud, the hypnosis, comes over the mind, and we believe ourselves to be separate. At some point in life, seeking occurs for that seemingly separate entity.

Then an understanding arises, and they are no longer in bondage to that.

Bob: What is all that you are talking about?

Q: That is the intelligence-energy.

Bob: No. What is all that you are describing? You are saying 'at some point, at some point, at some point'.

Q: It is the future.

Bob: Yes. So, where are you? You are in the imaginary concept of time!

Q: Yes.

Bob: What is time?

Q: Time is ... mind.

Bob: Mind! So, it is all mind stuff.

Q: But there is a perception of being in a cage, of suffering. You read these books. Sometimes you almost touch this freedom where there is no suffering.

Bob: There is a perception of the blue sky. There is a perception of the blue sea.

Q: Right.

Bob: But are they that?

Q: No, they are not that.

Bob: If you know that for certain, are you taken in by it?

Q: No.

Bob: You can still go and see it. You can't help but see it. But if somebody said, 'Go down and get a bucket of blue water out of the sea ...'

Q: ... *you couldn't do it.*

Bob: You couldn't do it. You wouldn't even think about it twice because that innate knowing, through the investigation, is there. It is the same with the blue in the sky or the water in the mirage.

Q: *There just hasn't been an innate knowing through investigation.*

Bob: Why hasn't there been?

Q: *As you say here, it just didn't ring a bell.*

Bob: If you look at it along those lines, can you find a centre or any separate entity there?

Q: *No. Only an idea, 'me'.*

Bob: An idea. Now, what is an idea?

Q: *It is a collection of memories.*

Bob: Yes, or thoughts. So, it is still the same thing. That 'me' is an image also. That is like the blue sea and the blue sky. You have got to see through that idea, too.

Q: *Yes.*

Bob: Whatever comes up can't be it!

Q: *Yes.*

Bob: In essence it is. That is what you have got to understand. It is one without a second. In essence it is, but not in the pattern or shape and form it is appearing as. All a thought is, is a pattern. The label is the shape and form that the vibration of energy has taken on. It has taken the shape and form of a word, the same as it has taken the shape and form of a body.

Q: *So, why the trick?*

Bob: You ask, 'Why the trick?' Just see through it. Instead of saying, 'It is all crap', see through the trick. But you want to know why the trick. You want to keep there, trying to find some solution to it, which you never will with thought.

Q: *Yes.*

Bob: It is all a trick or an imagined thing or an appearance. Why bother asking why? And who wants to know? It can only be something believing it is separate from that, that wants to know.

Q: *Yes. I get that.*

Bob: So, where does that leave you?

Q: *It leaves me right here, right now, aware of a mind that is trying to grasp onto something, but aware that it is …*

Bob: Right there, right now there is a presence of awareness. Full stop. Trying to grasp anything is more movement on it. It is a movement on that awareness-presence or presence-awareness, whichever way you like to put it. You can look at it both ways. There is awareness of presence. Or, there is awareness of the presence of awareness. That is basically all that there is, and all there ever is. Sometimes they use the analogy of a mirror. The mirror is self-shining and reflections appear in it. Is the mirror concerned whether or why there is a reflection there or not?

Q: *No, it isn't.*

Bob: Well, is awareness concerned?

Q: No.

Bob: It is only the idea in the mind that seemingly becomes concerned and wants to know, isn't it? So, when we ask the question, 'Who wants to know?', we are not having a go at you!

Q: No.

Bob: Ask yourself that question. Find out if there is any separate entity or anything with any personal volition or anything at all there that does want to know.

Q: Yes.

Bob: Even the question 'Who wants to know?' is just another pattern of energy appearing as that thought or pattern or shape and form of 'Who wants to know?'!

4. No Independent Existence

Bob: If you happen to grasp what I am saying right now, that is inquiring, because you are seeing where it all seemingly started from. You are seeing that there is no 'I' there that ever could do anything. From that time we started to reason, everything was acquired in the mind. It was all 'acquired mind' from then on. Through the acquisition of thoughts, words, images, ideas and by putting labels on things or conceptualizing, we built onto the 'I am' events, experience and conditioning. We formed a mental picture about ourselves, a mental concept of what we believe ourselves to be. Instead of having no reference point whatsoever, which would be the natural functioning, we formed this reference point, or the ego or self-centre. Everything from that time becomes relative to that. That is when you believe that 'you' have done this and done that or 'I'm not good enough' or whatever it is. But it is only a mental image. It has no power. Look and investigate now. See that it hasn't got any power. It has got no substance of its own. Try and grasp that 'I' thought. 'I', say it to yourself. Try and grasp hold of it. Try and make something substantial out of it.

Q: Yes.

Bob: Do these things, because that is the only way you will see.

Q: So, almost exaggerate it.

Bob: Yes! You will find that it has got no substance. Above all, it has got no independent existence. How many thoughts can you have if you are not conscious or aware?

Q: None.

Bob: So, it can't stand on its own. There is no 'I' or 'me' that can stand by itself apart from consciousness. It is really only a happening or an event in consciousness or awareness. It has no reality. We show you that constantly. We say 'You are seeing right now?' 'You are hearing right now?' Are your eyes saying 'I see'? Are your ears saying 'I hear'? But the thoughts 'I see' or 'I hear' come up to translate that seeing or hearing.

Q: *That conditioned mind ...*

Bob: Let me ask you this. Does the thought 'I see', can that see? The thought comes up, 'I see'. But can the thought, itself, see?

Q: *No.*

Bob: Can the thought 'I hear', hear? So, would the thought 'I am aware' be the awareness? Would the thought 'I am consciousness' be the consciousness?

Q: *No.*

Bob: It has got no power. So, the thoughts 'I'm going to do this' or 'I lost it' or 'I'm going to find it' haven't got any power whatsoever. But we are still habitually doing that.

Q: *I probably haven't listened to anything you just questioned, but my mind has come up with: 'If I have been beating myself up all day because I can't solve something or shift through something', my mind is now coming up with 'So, what to do?' That is probably what you just told me. I had a sense of peace after you said it, but now my mind has come back. (Laughter)*

Bob: So, 'What to do?' What does that imply?

Q: *That there is an 'I' wanting to do something.*

Bob: You are implying some future time when you will do

— 21 —

it. But ask yourself, question: 'What past is there, unless I think about it?' To do that, you have got to pause and just not think for a moment or an instant. Realize that there is not a past unless I think about it. And what future is there unless I think about it? From that you see that mind itself is time.

When you are thinking about anything, it is always presently. The actuality of it is presently. You can't think about the past in the past. Nor can you think about the future in the future. When you think about the past, you are thinking about the past right now. When you are thinking about the future, you are thinking about the future right now. So, you are really never away from presence. That is why they say it is omnipresence. That is all there is. You see from this that mind itself is time. The mind is thinking about past, and the mind is thinking about future. So, past and future are mental concepts.

When you say, 'What to do?', what have you done? You have subtly taken onboard that there is a future time when you will catch it, or watch it or it will drop away.

Q: ... and that there is a 'me' that has got all this stuff.

Bob: See how subtle it can be.

5. What is Thinking?

Q: *(Talking about being a seeker and a troubled person.)*

Bob: What is that?

Q: *A seemingly separate entity.*

Bob: Is it? What is it?

Q: *A collection of memories.*

Bob: So, it has got no power to do anything.

Q: *No.*

Bob: Do you see that, really see it?

Q: *No, I don't really see it. I hear it, but I live with the thing believing that it still has power.*

Bob: Have a look at your belief. Question it and see. What power could it have?

Q: *It has power of discursive thought, that I then believe is real.*

Bob: Has it got this discursive thought? What is doing the thinking? Is there a thinker, as such?

Q: *There seems to be a thinker.*

Bob: There seems to be. Have a look and see what that seeming thing is that seems to be! Have a look at it. There seems to be a thinker. Where or what is the thinker?

Q: *The mind.*

Bob: Yes. That is just thinking, isn't it?

Q: *That is thinking.*

Bob: When is it divided into 'thinker' and 'thought'?

Q: *It is always just thoughts, really.*

Bob: It is always just the thinking. That is the actuality. That is the activity that is going on. It is just the thinking. Now, what is thinking?

Q: *Thinking is energy coming through.*

Bob: All right. Do you think that energy can think? (*Laughs*)

Q: *No, but it can come together in forms that are thinking. It comes together in thoughts.*

Bob: … in thoughts. Yes.

Q: *So, it seems to be able to think.*

Bob: Seems to.

Q: *Thinking occurs.*

Bob: What is wrong with thinking occurring?

Q: *What is wrong with thinking occurring? What is wrong with that statement?*

Bob: Thinking is occurring. All right. Is there anything wrong with that?

Q: *Yes, because the thoughts get disturbed!*

Bob: How do you know? Isn't it split then into the thinker and the thought?

Q: *Yes. The thoughts are catching on something, this sense of 'I'.*

Bob: All right. What is this sense of 'I'? Have a look at that. If that is what it is catching on, that is your problem.

Q: *It is a point of view. It is just a point of view.*

Bob: A point of view, a reference point.

Q: *A reference point.*

Bob: Has that reference point got any substance? Is it something you can really grasp? Can you grasp that reference point and say, 'This is it. This is where I am'?

Q: *No!*

Bob: We don't look at it. When you really look at it and try to find something to grasp onto, you can't find it, can you? But we habitually believe it is there. So, it is seemingly very real—until it is questioned and looked at.

Q: *Yes.*

Bob: We immediately jump to the idea that 'I'm thinking'. We just take it for granted.

Q: *Then the thoughts relate to the reference point.*

Bob: Yes. The energy gives it a seeming reality.

Q: *(Second questioner) So, when there is a glimpse of something, when there is insight, (for want of a better word), when something is seen, there is no 'I' seeing it. What is actually happening? There is just seeing?*

Bob: Yes. There is just seeing. You have got to question. The only instrument we have got is the mind. Use the mind to question the mind. When it questions, it sees the falseness of itself. Like Ramana Maharshi says, you have got a thorn in your hand. So, you get another thorn off the tree, and you dig the first thorn out. Then you throw them both away.

Q: Right. So, it is a concept. It could be used to remove another concept.

Bob: As long as you understand that it is all conceptual. The concept is never the thing, is it?

Q: No.

Bob: Realize that all that is happening is conceptualization.

6. The Mirage

Bob: That separate entity, the belief in that entity or person, has never done a damn thing! It never can and never will. You must realize that you have been lived. That body-mind that you call 'you' is being lived, and it is being lived quite effortlessly. As Christ said, 'Which of you, by taking thought, can add one cubit to his stature?' That separate entity can't do a bloody thing.

Q: *What does that mean in terms of choice, conscious free-will, willing choices that people make or don't make? If I'm following you, there isn't anyone who makes the choice.*

Bob: No, there isn't. Choices are made, but there is no choice-maker. What seems to be choices are made. Like, you think you will do something, and you turn around doing something else. That is all coming from that pure functioning. But we take delivery of it and believe 'I am the choice-maker' or 'I have got free-will'. But we have just seen that if you look at it closely the thoughts 'I am' or 'I'm this or that' haven't got the power to do any of those things. You haven't even got the power to think that thought, itself. Thinking happens. It is the same with seeing. Seeing is happening right now. What do you have to do to see?

Q: *Nothing.*

Bob: It is spontaneously happening. Be that presence-awareness that is spontaneously happening of itself. It is effortless. If that 'I thought', that image you have about yourself, were running the show, what would be the most important thing you would do?

Q: *I have got no idea!*

Bob: Well, I do! The first thing I would do is make sure I take the next breath, or make sure my heart has got another beat in it. But all those things are happening quite effortlessly. We talk about choices. But if you are the choice maker, why would you ever have an unhappy thought, if you could choose your thoughts? Why would you ever be miserable or sad?

Q: *So, the intelligence-energy is vibrating into all these different forms.*

Bob: Exactly.

Q: *It is appearing as the chair, this life* (pointing to someone in the room), *this life, this life. What about the life of somebody who is suffering? Why would it do that? Why would it vibrate into the form of a life of a kid in a war-torn country? Do you know what I'm saying?*

Bob: Yes.

Q: *From my mind, I look at it and I say, 'That is madness'.*

Bob: Yes. It is madness. The intelligence-energy vibrates into the mirage, too. The heat shimmering off the road appears to be a pool of water. But what is it in actuality?

Q: *Just vibrating energy.*

Bob: Yes.

Q: *But that kid seems to suffer.*

Bob: Yes. But, as I say, you have got a million microbes crawling around your face right now.

Q: *You do that* (wipes hand on his face) *and you kill them all.*

Bob: You just wiped out a few million of them. Some of

them might be suffering. Some of them might be crippled. But you couldn't care less. We think we are so important, but we are only small in the scheme of things. Looking from out in space down on this earth what would you be? You would be even less than a microbe on someone's face! Yet, because we are here, we give ourselves so much importance. In the scheme of things, life is continually living on life. Life appears in all sorts of forms and shapes. But it is still the same life, the same intelligence-energy. And you are that life.

Q: *Does compassion fit into what you are saying?*

Bob: Yes, there is a natural compassion that comes up of itself. You don't have to try to *be* compassionate.

Q: *No.*

7. What is Realizing Itself?

Q: What is realizing itself?

Bob: That sense of presence expressing through the mind as the thought 'I am' is pure intelligence-energy. It is the knowing that you are. It is the activity of knowing. It is not the knower or the known, but that which you can't negate now—knowing. Knowing implies intelligence, doesn't it? And knowing is an actuality that is happening. It is an activity that is happening right in this instant. Any activity is a movement of energy. That activity of knowing is constantly there. The same intelligence-energy is functioning this universe. There is nobody out there moving the earth around the sun or making the seasons come and go or keeping the galaxies in their orbits or whatever they are doing. It implies that there is an intelligence there, doesn't it?

That innate intelligence is the essence of everything that appears and disappears. But to the mind it is no thing. It is no thing whatsoever. Look for yourself and try and see if you can negate it. Realize that you are aware of presence right now, of being present. You know that you are. What did you have to do for that to happen? It spontaneously arises. It is constantly, spontaneously, always and ever arising. The vibration, pulsation or throb of that intelligence is happening spontaneously. There is nothing to start it; nothing to stop it.

Q: So, there is nothing you have to do to settle down with it, then?

Bob: No. Realize there is no one to do it, and nothing to do, and it will settle down of its own accord. If energy doesn't go into a thing, it won't live. It can't live. There will be no fixating on anything. There will be no reference point, nothing accepted, nothing rejected, nothing attached to or detached from. These things will come up, but they won't last long. It is the very resistance to them, the trying to alter, modify or correct what is, that causes the conflict. The resistance to them is conflict, and conflict is dis-ease.

You can't practice non-resistance. You can say, 'I'm going to be non-resistant or attentive'. But you can't be, because there is no 'you' to do either. It is the recognition that is essential. The recognition that 'This is resistance' or 'This is inattention' must be from its opposite, from the point of non-resistance or the point of attention. In that very recognition, you are there in that instant, though it might only last a split second, initially. But it will come up again and you will recognize it, until you are constantly realizing these things, seeing these things. There will be times when you won't be. But you will know, the firm conviction will be there, that it is just like a cloud over the sky. No matter what is going on, that presence-awareness is still there. The sun is still in the sky, no matter how many clouds are over it. Then the fixation is not going into trying to disperse the clouds or worry about the clouds. The understanding or the recognition of that sun being there is enough. If there is no trying to alter, modify or correct the clouds, the cloud is going to disperse of its own accord, because that energy is not being resisted. It is going to move on. With the conflict or the resistance, the energy or concept or whatever it is is not being allowed to escape. So, it is thought in conflict with thought always. That is the cause of all of our problems.

8. Understanding the Mind

Q: *Bob, I have been thinking about something just lately, about understanding the mind. I think it is important to understand the mind. It is not like I understand it in detail, because the details are always different from moment to moment. But I feel like I'm getting a sort of a feel for what sort of things it does, the vanity and greed and all these things.*

Bob: What is that one heading that vanity, greed, self-pity, depression, anxiety, fear, etc. would come under?

Q: *Self-centre, I suppose?*

Bob: Self-centred activity. Exactly. Self-centred activity is the so-called 'me' or the ego. As we have seen, the 'me' or self-centre hasn't got any substance. When you investigate, there really is no such thing as a self-centre. So, investigate and understand fully that there is no self-centre. Then what would that activity apply to? Or could the activity happen?

Q: *Well, I assume that it would still go on, wouldn't it?*

Bob: But to whom? Who would be saying it is greed or fear or anger?

Q: *You wouldn't be labelling it, I suppose.*

Bob: No. The feeling will just be what is in the moment.

Q: *Yes.*

Bob: As soon as we label it with the past memory and past conditioning, that all gets downloaded onto it. That makes it worse than what it really is. If it is just what is (and 'what is' means it is unaltered, unmodified, uncorrected, just as it is) it won't stay there. The next thing that comes up, if that is unaltered, unmodified, uncorrected, and if the next thing that comes up is unaltered, unmodified, uncorrected, it means there is no one or nothing that has taken a stance anywhere. There is no reference point which these things can be referred to. It is just the natural flow.

But when it's referred to a reference point, that reference point discriminates what the other thing is: 'I don't like it because this thing happened to me before' or 'It is good, it is bad, it is pleasant, it is painful, I hate it, I love it' or whatever. As soon as those ideas come up, we try to alter, modify or correct what is. With that trying to alter, modify or correct what is there is a resistance to what is. Resistance is conflict, and conflict is dis-ease. If you are in conflict, you are uneasy. If you keep it there long enough it will mean disease. When we are resisting it, instead of being in the flow, it is like we have built a dam in the stream. What happens? The water builds up behind it until it spreads out over the banks or bursts the dam itself. Have a look at yourself at the emotions. If I'm resentful for instance, and I'm not getting it off of my chest, it is going to build up and burn away and burn away. There is certainly dis-ease there. I am not at ease. It is going to be taken out in anger or some other form. It is going to erupt.

It is good that you are looking at the mind. That is needed. You need to understand it. You don't need to get bogged up in the finer points of it. Just to see that basically there is no such thing as mind apart from thought.

Q: Yes.

Bob: The thoughts that are happening. We bunch them all together and call it 'mind'. But it is only thoughts. And thoughts are subtle words, because we generally think in words or images. At the spoken level, it is sound. Sound is a vibration. Vibration is a movement of energy. That is all the so-called mind is. It is energy, formed into patterns, as this particular thought, the table, chair, bird, dog, me, you, car, or whatever. These are all patterns of energy. The particular pattern or how it is appearing is not the reality of it. Its reality is energy. We take how it is appearing to be real, rather than seeing through to the essence of it. And we get bound in the appearance.

The ideas that we have about ourselves, such as 'I'm John', 'I'm Bill', 'I'm not good enough', 'I have got low self-esteem' and so on are mental images. I am bound in that mental image because it is believed in. The energy has gone into that belief, that idea of a 'me' also.

Understand that this body is a pattern also. Basically, it is made up of the elements. It is made up of earth, water, fire, air and space. All those elements can be broken down into subatomic particles, which are basically energy. So, it is a pattern of energy, whirling at a terrific pace that seemingly keeps it solid. It is the same with that chair. It seems solid. Or take the case of a propeller blade turning at so many revolutions per minute. It appears to be a solid circle. Stick your finger in it and see what happens to it! (*Laughs*)

Q: Do you consider your body just the same as that chair?

Bob: Yes. Well, I don't make any discrimination between them. I understand it to be what it is. It is here as a so-called body. It has all the pains, aches, feeling well or whatever goes on in the body, exactly like it did before. But it is not what I really am. The essence of it is what I really am, but not how it is appearing. If it was how it is appearing, it is constantly changing. It is transient. There are hundreds of millions of cells breaking down in it and being replaced right now. It is constantly renewing. So, how can I say, 'I am the body'?

Q: Bob, that is an issue that I'm struggling with. We have this scientific knowledge that we are not the body, because we know it is energy. But if you didn't have that knowledge, is there some more immediate reason why we are not the body, a reason which doesn't require you to go off and think, 'well, it is this and that and the other'?

Bob: In investigating it, breaking it down like I just did, questioning your belief that you are the body, seeing it in whatever way you can, seeing conclusively that you can't be the body, then it is immediate. You can never take it on again, though it goes through all the activities of a so-called body. But you know the truth about it.

Q: *The trouble is that I know the truth about it. I mean, I have had scientific training. I know it is just atoms and atoms are energy, and it is all basic space. But it seems so real to me in my everyday living that that information doesn't seem to be as powerful as the information that I get from my senses.*

Bob: What do you mean 'the information you get from your senses'? Do you mean that there is pain here or something seemingly solid here? Again, have a look at a lot of other things beside the body that are seemingly solid, too.

Q: *It is quite hard with the conditioning that we have had for years ... I know you will say 'Hard for who?'! (Laughter)*

Bob: Yes. That is why I say the old patterns, the habit patterns, the so-called conditioning is there. That has been believed in for so long. But question it a few times. It is the same with that chair here. It seems pretty solid. Say you are a cabinet maker or something. There are a few pieces of wood there, a bit of cloth, a few nails, and a bit of glue. From that perspective, you couldn't call it a chair, could you?

Q: *No. What are you getting at?*

Bob: When it is broken down, it was a tree at one stage, apart from other things. The same with the body.

Q: *Would it be something like, because I'm aware of the body, I can't be the body because something is aware of it?*

Bob: Yes. Innately, you know that too. You are constantly saying 'my' body, 'my' mind. If you really believed you were the body or you really were the body, you would say 'I-body' or 'I-mind', wouldn't you? It is just like saying 'my' coat, 'my' car. You own or possess those things. When you say 'my' body, 'my' mind, who is the owner or possessor?

Q: There is no owner.

Q: (Second questioner) That all made sense for me on Tuesday night with the mirror analogy.

Bob: Yes.

Q: For some reason, I got this concept that I was the mirror, and I was everything appearing in the mirror. The appearances weren't real, but the essence was real. I was the mirror and everything appearing in it. Everything was appearing in it. Now I have lost that. I mean, I know it was a concept. I remember saying to myself, 'This is just a concept, but this will do for a minute because it is better than my other concept of an "I"or "me".'

Bob: But what resonated with you in the very seeing of it, you haven't lost that?

Q: The understanding of that analogy I haven't lost.

Bob: Yes. When it made sense for you, you saw it.

Q: I saw it, yes.

Bob: You saw that is was the one essence which everything was appearing on.

Q: Yes.

Bob: You regarded yourself as that essence at the time.

Q: Well, yes.

Bob: To the mind, that essence is no thing.

Q: Yes.

Bob: When you try and grasp 'no thing', you will lose it. But if you saw that, you understand that that essence, like the mirror, has never been contaminated by anything that has appeared in it.

Q: Yes. That was very strong. But it is gone.

Bob: The concept might have gone, but has the essence itself gone?

Q: The essence can't go.

Bob: So, the concept you had about it was just another appearance in the mirror. But you, being the mirror, are aware of it coming and going.

Q: Yes! The self-centre doesn't like this notion of emptiness, though.

Bob: No.

Q: It doesn't like it at all.

Bob: It can't grasp no thing. Understand what it is—it is a thought.

Q: 'No thing' is a thought?

Bob: No. The self-centre is a thought, an image.

Q: Yes.

Bob: You are aware of thinking, aren't you?

Q: Yes.

Bob: So, you are aware of thoughts. Thoughts are things.

You are aware of the cars going by. You are aware of the chair. You are aware of the table. You are aware of all those things. Realize that you are that which is aware of these things. They are things. Thought itself, being a thing, can't understand no thing. That is why you will never grasp it with the mind. The answer is not in the mind. It can't be.

Q: *If it is beyond the mind, the mind can't grasp that which is beyond the mind.*

Bob: No, it can't. It contains the mind. The mind can never contain it. That is why it says in the Gita, 'The sword can't cut it, the fire can't burn it, the water can't drown it, and the wind can't dry it'. You can't grasp it with a thought. But can you negate that beingness? Under any circumstances can you say you are not? But what that beingness is you cannot conceptualize. For the sake of terms, we will use the terms 'awareness' or 'consciousness' or 'truth' or 'reality' or 'God' or 'spirit'. All these are concepts we use, trying to point to it. But none of them are ever it. Yet you cannot negate that knowing that you are, that essence of beingness that you are. And you can't grasp it either. That is what you really are. That is not separate. It is one only, solely.

Q: *It is the sound of one hand clapping!* (Laughter) *I guess the goal of spiritual pursuit is to be there, wherever 'there' is.*

Bob: Yes, but the point is, it is not 'there'. It is here and now, omnipresent. What do you have to do to be aware?

Q: *Nothing.*

Bob: It is spontaneously arising, ceaselessly arising, ever fresh, ever new.

Q: *If you experience it, then you don't know that.*

Bob: If you experience it, it wouldn't be it. Anything that is experienced is not it. So, people look for silence and stillness.

— 38 —

They think that is it. But those are experiences. What you are is the experiencing, which all these things are happening on. It is just like seeing. The seeing is happening. But when we split the seeing up into 'I see the chair', we split seeing up into the seer that says 'I see' and the thought or idea that says 'I see'. That becomes the pseudo-subject, and the chair becomes the object. But they are both contained in the seeing. Because, can there be a seer without seeing? Can there?

Q: Can there be the seer without seeing? I don't know!

Bob: Well, have a look at it. There can't be a seer without seeing, nor can there be the seen without seeing.

Q: So, you need seeing for both.

Bob: You need seeing for both. They are both two ends of seeing, like a seesaw or set of scales. The actuality is the seeing, and it is seemingly divided into the seer and the seen. As soon as the thought comes up 'I see', know that that is only the translation, instead of seeing that as a belief that there is a seer. The thought 'I see the chair' is another label, another concept. The thought 'I see' is a thought, and the thought 'the chair' is a thought. So, the seer and the seen are the same thing, both vibrations, both movements of thought. But the actuality is the seeing.

You can see that right now. Turn your head to the left quickly. Back again. What did you see?

Q: Mirror? Curtain?

Bob: You saw more than that. Realize that you saw everything. But you can only label, you can only remember or label with the mind 'mirror', 'curtains' and a couple of other things. But realize that everything is being registered, just like a camera taking a picture. It is the same with hearing. You are hearing me, but you are hearing those cars going by, too. You are hearing lots of other sounds in the room. It is all being registered as it is, but we think what we are seeing

— 39 —

is only what we label. It is happening spontaneously and effortlessly. It is all being registered just as it is. And just as it is, it is not a problem. But instead of leaving it just as it is, we say 'that is a chair', 'that is a so and so', etc. 'What is' means unaltered, unmodified, uncorrected. When we see something and say 'That is a chair', 'I don't like it', 'I don't like the colour', we are trying to alter or modify or correct what is. With that comes resistance. We are resisting what is. Resistance is conflict, and conflict is dis-ease. When that resistance or conflict is going on, you are not at ease. You are no longer relaxed and at ease. Not being relaxed and at ease is dis-ease. Keep that dis-ease there long enough and it will manifest as disease in the body.

Realize that even these words are bubbling out of here. I'm not thinking what I'm going to say next!

Q: Bob, the seer and the seen are thoughts, but the seeing is not a thought. That is the difference. The being is not a thought. Presence is not a thought. The mind splits it all into words and everything, and that is what we seemingly live in. This entity lives in these thoughts and things. But it is not real.

Bob: No, it is not. The mind is just really a translator, a translator of what is coming up. I use the analogy of putting a piece of iron in the fire. It'll get red like fire. It'll get hot like fire. Pick it up, and it'll burn you like fire. So, it has taken on the qualities of the fire. If it was like our minds, it would say 'Look at me! Look what I can do; I'm red; I'm hot; I can burn!' But take it out of the fire, and what can it do? It can't do any of those things. It is the same with thinking. Thinking is so closely aligned to that pure intelligence that it has come to believe that it is the intelligence itself . It thinks, 'I choose' or 'I have got will' or 'I can do this' or 'I'm not good enough' or 'I am an evil person' or whatever. But all thought really does, when you look at it closely, is translate. When you question it and look at it, you can see that of itself it hasn't got any power. It hasn't got any substance or independent nature. In seeing that and realizing that, then what does the mind do? It just aligns itself with that intelligence. It just translates from that, instead of taking the belief that it has some power or some sense of entity and separateness of itself.

Q: So, you think yourself out of thought. I mean that is the awareness. As the awareness grows, you think yourself out of thought.

Bob: But you can't do it with the thought. That is why I say you can never find the answer in the mind. That is what we have believed we could do all the time. You can never find the answer for life in the mind because, as we said before, it is prior to the mind. The mind can't contain it or grasp it. It contains the mind.

Q: How do you go beyond the mind?

Bob: You don't go beyond the mind. You are beyond it right now.

Q: That is right!

Bob: But realize that right now you are present and aware, first and foremost. That is prior to any thought. Realize that that is ceaselessly and spontaneously arising, prior to any thought. You are beyond the mind. Realize that.

You are an intelligent person. You found the answer to a lot of things through working them out in the mind. But you never found the answer to this. Now, wouldn't you conclude after a while, 'I haven't found the answer yet, and I'm not a dummy. Maybe I'm looking in the wrong direction. Maybe the answer is not there'? As soon as you have come to that conclusion, you stop seeking for something that you already are. You just relax into it, and it reveals itself to you.

Q: Is that part of that concept of surrender, for want of a better word?

Bob: Yes. But that is a trap, too, because there is a belief that there is somebody there who can surrender. You have got to watch all the subtleties of this.

Q: *It is very subtle.*

Bob: But you start to catch them after a while, and you don't fall into the traps.

Q: *I have this big thing of, 'OK, now that I have left Bob's, what should I do with all this?' I remember reading about someone saying, 'Just do nothing. Forget everything I have said. That is the best thing you can do, because you are just dragging it from the past'. I'm just talking to myself here.* (Laughter)

Bob: Ask yourself, 'Who is asking the question?' That must be 'me'. Then you recall, 'That idiot up there says there is no me. Is he right or is he wrong? I'll have a look'. Then have a look and try to find where this 'me' you believe yourself to be is. See if you can find it.

Q: *That is the only way, to keep having a look.*

Bob: Yes. Until the firm conviction is there that there is no place here that you can call the centre or reference point. There is nothing substantial or with any independent nature that I can point to and say, 'This is where I begin, this is what I really am'.

Q: *If you don't look, it is like taking your teaching on faith or something. You have got to look.*

Bob: You have to see for yourself. Nobody can do it for you.

9. The Word is not the Real

Bob: The cage of self-centredness, which I have built around myself, a cage of words, is a phantom. It is a ghost. It does not exist. The cage door is open right now. As a matter of fact, the whole cage is there and can be seen for what it is and fall away right now.

The cage of limitation. Words! Good/bad, pleasant/painful, positive/negative, possible/impossible. All words! But the word is not the real. Grasp that one also. You can say 'water, water, water' for the rest of your life. Try and drink the word! A word is a symbol for something. It is not the real. Yet when I say 'I'm no good' or 'I have got low self-esteem' or 'I'm feeling so and so', what reality have those words got? Or when you say, 'I'm superior', 'I'm better' – is that what you are? What does that symbolize? Can it be there at all if there were no beingness, if there were no livingness?

Instead of trying to come up with an answer in the mind, wouldn't it be wise to just be with this livingness, to settle down with this beingness, this presence? Watch it; be aware or be alert to how it is expressing; feel it shining through your eyes, lighting up your face, how it can twist it into a frown or a smile; feeling the breath. In that seeing, in that light that is shining out of your eyes, marvel at the very fact of seeing. Just see it as it is, in all the variety and diversity that it can express. Marvel at all the different feelings, instead of attaching to them and allowing them to build up till they've grown out of all proportion, till they've taken over the whole of that awareness and functioning to the exclusion of everything else.

What is wrong with right now, unless you think about it? There is an instant pause while you are trying to look to see what is wrong. Realize that before anything can be wrong, there has got to be thought. Come back to that constantly.

Right here, right now, presently, there is nothing wrong, unless I think about it. What past is there, unless I think about it? What future is there, unless I think about it?

10. Primal Mind

Bob: What has got to be grasped is this awareness. It is not that it has to be 'grasped'. The primal mind or primal awareness has got to be understood. It is like the little child. The little child is not self-aware till he is about two years old. There was a video program about the body in which this was very obvious. The little child was about eighteen months or two years old. They put him before a mirror. They put a little dot of red paint on his nose. The little child was not saying, 'Oh, look, I have got a red dot on my nose'. He doesn't associate what is in the mirror with what he is at all. There is no self-awareness. There is awareness there. This is what we call the 'primal mind' or the 'primal awareness'. There is awareness, and that awareness is constant. He is registering everything that is going on around him and all the rest of it. He is even seeing the face in the mirror, but he is not self-aware. This is our problem. We believe we are this entity. That is when this idea of self-awareness comes upon us. That is what obscures the primal awareness. The intelligence-energy that is growing the body and doing the livingness has always been there. It is happening right now in the immediacy of right now.

You can all drop the sense of self right now. Realize, get a glimpse of that primal awareness that is registering every-thing. You are still hearing everything. Seeing is still hap-pening. If you move your toe or your foot, there is doing still happening. This is what this is all about: the natural state, not the acquired state. When you started to reason, from that time on, everything you know from then on has been acquired or learned. Even the thought 'I am' is acquired. You haven't got that thought prior to that. You haven't got a word for it till you hear these words. You haven't got a name or a label for anything. Then we start learning, and we are acquiring everything from then on. But the functioning, the primal activity is what is living you and breathing you, beating your heart, growing your fingernails, and even doing the thinking. But all the activity is happening by itself.

Q: Could we say the moment and content of moment without naming it, that is what is actual?

Bob: That is what is the actual. If you look at it further, you see that even the content, when it is broken down, is just a movement of energy also. It is all just a vibration of energy, a movement of energy. We give the shape and form that it is appearing in a label, a name.

Q: When you first started talking, you said, 'What has to be grasped, or not grasped but understood...' That is an interesting point there. What needs to understand? Is it the ordinary mind that has to align itself?

Bob: It has to be seen that, primarily, there is this pure intelligence-energy or awareness, not the self-awareness. That is the difference. Everything that arises from that time on is referenced to that self-awareness. From then on, it is either for the improvement or detriment of that self-awareness. That is the problem.

11. What's Wrong with Right Now?

Bob: *(Referring to his first book of dialogues)* The title of the book is *What's Wrong with Right Now, Unless You Think About It?* To do that, you have got to pull up and stop thought. Even stop it for a second, for an instant. You realize there is not a thing you can say about it. But you can't deny the fact that it still is as it is. As it is, you can't say it is good, bad, pleasant or anything. It is just what is. 'What is' means it is unaltered, unmodified, uncorrected. It is just like a camera that will take a picture of everything in this room, just as it is. It doesn't say 'I don't want that' or 'I'll have that bit in. That is more pleasant than the other'. It is just taking it as it is. This is what is happening in the functioning with you right now. It is always as it is. But then it is referred to the 'me' of memory. From there it is altered, modified or corrected with some preference, partiality or comparison. All problems arise from that.

   It doesn't mean to say that these things won't go on. They'll go on. But you have got to see this clearly and understand it. With the understanding of it, let it go on. But there is no longer anyone or anything to be bound by it. Before, in believing it, there is that bondage to it. The bondage of self is there. That bondage is our problem. That is our conflict. That is a resistance to what is.

12. Knowing without a Concept

Q: Can there be knowing without a concept?

Bob: Yes! That is happening with you right now, in the immediacy of right now. You are knowing that you are. Look around the room, as I say. Look around the room quickly and realize that before you conceptualize anything it is being registered first.

Q: But before that, you were saying that awareness can't be changed or modified, and it is the only one. But then to be able to say that, you need a concept. I mean, there has got to be some concept that this awareness can't be changed or modified. Prove to me that it can't be changed or modified, without using a concept.

Bob: You prove it to yourself! Go back into your memory. Has that essence or awareness that you are ever changed?

Q: But that awareness is a concept.

Bob: We are using a term, but you know what I'm talking about—that knowing that you are, that subtle beingness or livingness. From the time that you can first remember, has that ever changed? Is it scarred by the dramas or traumas? Is it hurt? Does it have any 'poor me' about it? Does it have any anxiety or anything else?

Q: I can't answer that without making it into some sort of concept.

Bob: Yes. But you don't have to answer it. Just know for yourself. See it. Is it any different now? What is the very first thing you are seeing or registering?

Q: *That is the space.*

Bob: Space. Is that space clear? Is there anything in it, in the immediacy of where you are seeing from?

Q: *What do you mean by 'clear'?*

Bob: There are objects further out. But what is right where you first think you are seeing?

Q: *It just seems to be dark or clear, if you want to call it that. Empty.*

Bob: There is nothing in it. It is clear and empty. Have a look at that.
  All throughout the day, up through right now, through all the dramas and traumas, looking back there instantly, is there ever a thought there, is there ever an entity there? Is there ever anything there at all?

13. The Search is the Trap

Bob: The search itself is the trap. You are already what you are seeking. You think there is something to attain or to get. You have never been anything other than that, and never could be. We hear that, but how many of us really take a good look at it and stick with it, hang onto it? What do we do? 'That is not good enough!' We will race away and look at somebody else. We will go to somebody else, hear somebody else, read another book or do this or do that, thinking we will get the answer somewhere else. But the only place the answer is, is with you. It is not with anybody else. You already are that. You can't be anything else other than that.

Any questions?

Q: *The basic consciousness is the separation, because as soon as the consciousness starts, the separation has started. 'I am' is the separation.*

Bob: Yes. That sense of self becomes the sense of separation. The sense of separation brings with it insecurity and vulnerability.

Q: *I'm using the word 'consciousness'. Should I say 'basic awareness' is the separation?*

Bob: It doesn't matter what concept you use! There are millions of different concepts for it. With the concept, with the words, we can only point at it. We can only point you to where to look. But it is something that cannot be grasped with a word, because the word is never the thing.

Have a look. If that sense of presence wasn't there, if you weren't that, could there be consciousness or could there be mind or awareness or whatever you would like to divide it into? They say it is unborn. Unborn means not originated.

There is no origin to it. It wasn't created. It had no beginning. So, you can't really say it is or it is not. It is self-arising and ceaselessly arising. It is futile to try to clutch onto it or latch onto it with a concept or a word or an idea or a thought. But, basically, you can't get out of it.

14. Is There Awareness There?

Q: Somehow, what we have talked about hasn't struck home. I don't seem to have abandoned the 'I'. It hasn't been challenged substantially or cut away at the knees. That needs to be challenged, it seems.

Bob: Drop everything we have talked about and thought about.

Q: OK.

Bob: Is there awareness here now?

Q: Yes.

Bob: Full stop?

Q: Yes.

Bob: We immediately want to rush into the thought or the thinking because that awareness is no thing to the mind. The mind is full of sensations and reasoning, and this, that and the other. The mind is displaying in one way or another with thoughts, feelings and emotions. But cut all that away. It is clear; it is empty; it is lucid; and it is really vibrating there, pulsating through you right now as that livingness.

Q: All of us are experiencing that awareness. Well, we are that awareness now.

Bob: You are that awareness.

Q: Thought comes and goes. We are all thinking and talking about what is going on here, but none of it at the moment is being referred to the self-centre, necessarily. But thought still happens.

Bob: Yes, of course! The cars still go by! They are registered. There are movements in the room. There are sights, sounds, hearing and feeling. You might move your foot, or feel your backside on the seat. It is all still functioning.

Q: A lot of that was being referred to a self-centre before I came in here. The first five minutes I hadn't settled down. The mind hadn't really gotten fully involved in all this. I was still thinking about the trip up here, and whether it would have been better to have come this way, rather than that way. The mind was still thinking about that, using memory, and referring it to a 'me' there, I suppose. But now the mind seems involved with what awareness is looking at.

Bob: Yes. That is what needs to happen. The focus needs to be from knowing that you are that awareness, instead of focusing out there on what has been appearing on that mind and all the rest. That is what we are conditioned to do. Just come back to what you really are. Come back to that awareness, which is no thing. Realize that; expand that; and you realize that it is just like the metaphor of space. To grasp the car, where do you go? Does the sound come to you? Is there some particular thing where sound comes to? If you are looking here, you can't even see a head or ears! But the hearing is happening. If you investigate, there is more space around that sound. There is the vastness of space. The vastness of awareness is similar to the space. It is encompassing all those sounds, not 'out there' or 'in here', but just the pure hearing or the pure functioning of it.

Q: How is it that one isn't satisfied with that?

Bob: You are not satisfied with it because it is very subtle. We are used to the sensations. That is why we continue to look 'out there' for bigger and better sensations. Or we imagine there is some strange big bang or something that happens with enlightenment or realization. We think, 'In the future

I'll attain it or I'll get it'. There is all sorts of imagination of what it will be like. That is what we continue to look for. We never stop with it. But stay with the subtleness of it.

Q: Well, yes.

Bob: As Nisargadatta says, 'My silence sings; my emptiness is full'. And it does. You can feel it vibrating through you and pulsing through you, very subtly. It is a sense of joy, a sense of well-being, not a highly emotional state that is going to burn you out. You can't stay highly emotional. It is just the same as if you stay angry and stressful long enough, you get disease. Likewise if you are in some ecstatic state. You will burn out also. Stay with the subtleness of that, the vibrancy of that, and you will start to realize what it is really like. Nothing can touch you from there. Without any sense of person there, just being, just sitting there being right now, drop all ideas of 'I'. What can you say about it without going in your mind?

Q: I can't say anything about it!

Bob: You can't say anything without a thought. But, you are hearing?

Q: Oh, yes.

Bob: You are seeing?

Q: Yes.

Bob: So, the functioning is still happening without any mental image.

Q: That is right.

Bob: There is an awareness or sense of presence there. What do you need to do to acquire that?

Q: *Oh, well, you don't, do you!*

Bob: You don't. It is there of itself, self-arising, self-knowing, timelessly and ceaselessly. Without a thought, what conditioning is there? (*Pause*)

Go back to that. Without a thought, you are just that pure seeing, pure hearing, pure functioning. Isn't that so?

Q: *Yes.*

Bob: Where is your conditioning apart from thinking?

Q: *There isn't any.*

Bob: That is right! People want to analyze and get rid of their conditioning. The way to get rid of your conditioning is: full stop. Full stop! Right here, right now, without thinking about it, there is no conditioning whatsoever. Just come back and settle with that. See the truth, see the fact of that. Be the fact of that.

It is futile trying to clutch onto it or latch onto it with a concept or word or an idea or a thought. But, basically, you can't get out of it. You can go back in the past as far as you like, or anticipate or imagine the future as far as you like; you can create for yourself a heaven or hell in the mind or a realization or an enlightenment or a resurrection; you can create all these things in the mind. But have you ever left that presence-awareness?

15. The Concept of Time

Bob: All right. You have all been here. You all know the basics of it. What did you get? Have you got all the answers?

Q: No. I don't think I have got all the answers. But I suppose in time you sort of understand different things, slowly, slowly.

Bob: Well, you have got that concept of time. Slowly, slowly can go on forever, can't it?

Q: It could, yes.

Bob: What's wrong with right now if you are not thinking about it?

Q: Right now is just fine.

Bob: Grasp that. Right now is fine without thinking about it. You must realize from that, that thought is the only problem you can have, isn't it?

Q: Yes.

Bob: You have been here before, and you have heard that what you are seeking you already are. If you go around here, there and everywhere trying to get something, it is a futile effort.

Q: You have to go around here and there to find out that you don't need to.

Q: (Second questioner) Yes, you do! Most people do. You go shopping to find all the stuff you don't need.

Q: (First questioner) *Well, different people put it different ways.*
You can understand different things from different people.

Bob: Yes, but are you aware right now? You are aware of presence?

Q: *I'm aware right now.*

Bob: So, do you think it is any more than that?

Q: *That is it.* (Laughs)

Bob: Yes. That is it!

Q: *But …*

Bob: But what?

Q: *Well, the next minute, I'll be caught up in … stuff.*

Bob: But can you live that next minute now?

Q: *No.*

Bob: So, in the now, you are projecting about a future time when you will be caught up in it. See how you trap yourself?

Q: *Yes. It is based on past experience, isn't it?*

Bob: Yes. That becomes the reference point. We refer to everything from that past experience. But that is already dead now. You can't live the next minute right now. You can't live the past minute or past years or anything past right now. You might recall them. In recalling them, they are not the actual thing that happened, are they? They are only a recollection of them, which your mind has embellished a bit or forgotten part of. It is not actually as it was.

Q: In my work, I need to reflect on things sometimes.

Bob: In that way, you are using memory. Memory is there and you think, 'I guess I'll do it this way'. You are using memory. But the other way, memory is using you. You think, 'I haven't got it' or 'I have to get something' or 'I'm no good' or whatever. That is when it puts the limitations and boundaries on you.

Q: Say, while you are reflecting on something, you think, 'Oh gosh, I shouldn't have done that'.

Bob: Have a look at it. You recall something and you say, 'I shouldn't have done it'. But, can you change it? Why beat yourself up about what you could have, should have, shouldn't have done? Realize that there is no personal doer of it. Who was the 'you', the idea, the entity that could or could not do it?

Q: It is really hard to get that concept of no one being there, along with, say, next time I won't do that, so I adjust my behaviour in the future. I really find it hard to let go of the thought that I had a bit of control there.

Bob: Have a look at it. You are seeing right now?

Q: Am I seeing?

Bob: Yes. You are seeing everything around you?

Q: Around the room, you mean?

Bob: Yes. You are hearing this voice? Other things? Are your eyes saying to you, 'I see'?

Q: My actual eyes aren't, no.

Bob: Are your actual ears saying, 'I hear'?

Q: No. But my brain is.

Bob: Oh, is it! Can your brain give you any thought at all? Is your brain saying 'I think'?

Q: It is happening in there. (Points to her head)

Bob: Is it?

Q: It feels like it.

Bob: Is it? Have a look and see if you can find out where it is happening. These are the things you have got to look at, you know. Whereabouts is it happening in there?

Q: It could be happening out there somewhere or ...

Bob: Never mind trying to conceptualize or hypothesize where it could be happening. Have a look and see where your thoughts are happening in there.

Q: I imagine it travels along a little neuron. (Laughs) A few of them come together and ... ooh!

Q: (Second questioner) Bob, when you close your eyes and you look for it, it still feels like it is coming from your head.

Bob: Does it?

Q: That is what you imagine. Yes.

Bob: All right. If that is what you imagine, where are you imagining it from?

Q: Oh! Nowhere! (Laughs)

Bob: That just shows that there is no centre or reference point that is really concrete. There is no place you can point to and say, 'This is where it all is'.

Q: Yes!

Bob: All the brain is, is an instrument that breaks down that pure intelligence-energy. It is like a transformer in a record player or something. Instead of playing at 240 volts, it breaks it down to 12 volts. Otherwise, it would blow it apart. The brain is just transforming that intelligence-energy into thoughts. It is not thinking.

Q: It is just a transmitter.

Bob: Yes! It is just the same as your kidneys, your liver, and your heart and all the rest of it. It is the intelligence-energy going through them that is allowing them to do their job, to do what they're meant to do. The brain doesn't think.

Go back to the seeing. Does the thought 'I see', does that see?

Q: Does the thought see?

Bob: Yes.

Q: No.

Bob: The eye doesn't say, 'I see'. The ear doesn't say, 'I hear'. The thought 'I see', which is translating what is happening, doesn't see. The thought 'I hear' doesn't hear. Those thoughts are just translating what is happening, the actual functioning. You are constantly seeing, even while you are listening to what I'm saying. Nothing is there saying 'I'm seeing, I'm seeing, I'm seeing' while you are listening to me, is there?

Q: No.

Bob: But the seeing is happening. Nothing is saying, 'I'm hearing, I'm hearing, I'm hearing' while you are looking around the room. You are still hearing the cars go by. That seeing and hearing, that functioning, is happening before the thought. If you look, the thought 'I see' can't see. The thought 'I hear' can't hear. The thought 'I am aware' is not the awareness. Is it?

Q: No.

Bob: The thought 'I think' is not the thinking.

Q: No.

Bob: So, the thought 'me' is also just a translation. It is just not what you really are. That 'me', that image that you have got about yourself, 'I am so and so' and 'I do this' and all the rest of it, the image you have about yourself hasn't got one jot of power to do anything. That is the self-image or self-centre you have about yourself.

Q: It is really just hard to sort of make sense then why we ever do anything. Well, we have got to feed ourselves so that our body stays alive.

Bob: But, that is the point! It is hard to say why we ever do anything? You don't do anything. Have a look. Go back before that thinking was happening, as far back as you remember. When do you start to remember? At about two or three years old? Prior to that, you were just functioning, spontaneously and effortlessly. The natural state is just going on; everything is going on quite naturally. From then on, everything is acquired or learned. That is what I call the 'acquired mind'. But prior to that, the natural state is functioning.

Now, you are breathing right now. If you were in control of it, the first thing you would be saying is 'Let me make sure I take my next breath', 'make sure my heart has got another beat in it', 'make sure I am able to digest my food and replace the cells in the body'. But why don't you think of any of those things? Aren't they happening effortlessly and spontaneously? It is just the same as a thought arising. It arises effortlessly and spontaneously. Then you believe or think that 'I' choose my thoughts or create that thought. It has got no power to do any of those things. To that 'I' thought we add events and experiences and form a mental picture of what we believe we are. It is only a mental image based on past events and experiences.

Q: We have all got different past experience.

Bob: Yes. So, you form the image around that. 'Oh, I can't do that' or 'I shouldn't be doing this'. This depends on what we consider as good or bad, which is based on past events and experience. That is the only way you can judge it. That mental picture is what we call the self-centre or the ego. But it is powerless of itself. If that intelligence-energy, that life force, that livingness wasn't there, how many thoughts could you have?

Q: Probably none. You would be dead.

Bob: Yes. You wouldn't have any thoughts, would you? You wouldn't have any thoughts. You wouldn't have any feelings. You wouldn't have any emotions. None of that would be there. That thinking that you believe to be you hasn't got any independent nature.

Q: It is just like you said of memories that you have. That is what you base your future upon. A thought will come and depending on what your past experiences are, you will sort of …

Bob: … judge it as good or bad, pleasant or painful, I like it or I don't like it, I want it or I don't want it. You refer to that reference point, which is a dead image based on the past. From there, it is believed to be so. But realize that thought has come up spontaneously, effortlessly and intuitively. If it is acted on in the moment, before it is referred to the 'me' of past memory, your life would be probably a lot more effortless and easy. But we have learned to disregard that spontaneous functioning and refer it to the 'me' of memory.

Q: I won't dive into a shallow pool because my past experience tells me that it is not a good idea.

Bob: Yes. That is intelligence.

Q: But it is the same thing as anything else, isn't it?

Bob: Yes. But there is not a personal doer there.

16. You Are the Functioning

Bob: How is it going, Robert?

Q: I'm still struggling with the idea of questioning my beliefs as a way into this oneness. I feel quite in tune with the idea that we trick ourselves with thought and get swallowed up in it or think that it is 'me' making the decisions. But how do I get beyond that? I can't stop thinking. I can question what I'm thinking, if I'm aware enough to do it or strong enough or not in the pit of despair and thinking that I can't do anything.

Bob: Yes. All right. You are thinking right now?

Q: Yes.

Bob: What is thinking appearing on?

Q: What is it appearing on? In my mind. I suppose, what I call my mind is where it appears. In my head.

Bob: Does it appear in your head or you mind? Have you had a look? Question that and have a look.

Q: Where does my thought appear? Thoughts go on in my head.

Bob: This is what we are questioning. Just take a guess at it, as we say. Whereabouts in your head? Can you pin-point it, exactly?

Q: No. It sort of floats away!

Bob: You take it for granted it is in your head. Are you aware of thought taking place?

Q: I am aware of thought, yes.

Bob: All right. What is it that is aware of thought?

Q: I'm aware of thought. What is aware of those thoughts? Well, I, me.

Bob: 'I', 'me'—those are thoughts.

Q: Yes.

Bob: Before that, before you said that, you are aware.

Q: I'm aware of things other than thoughts, I suppose.

Bob: Yes.

Q: But I am not aware unless I think about them.

Bob: If you are not thinking, do you fall apart?

Q: No.

Bob: Why?

Q: It is not my thoughts holding me together!

Bob: Right. If it is not your thoughts holding you together, that means there is something there prior to thought.

Q: Yes?

Bob: You just said you have got to get prior to thought.

Q: Yes?

Bob: Relax in that. Don't try to 'nut it out' with the mind, because you will never grasp it with the mind. It is no thing. This is where the mind balks at it. It is no thing that you can grasp or conceptualize. All the mind, all that thought, can do is make a concept, an image or a label. It can't even understand or grasp anything.

Q: *I can contemplate what is there in me that is prior to thought. Not even in me, just what is there prior to thought.*

Bob: If I ask you, 'What's wrong with right now, if you are not thinking about it?', you have got to pause thought for a moment to have a look, don't you? Well, pause thought for a moment. What can you say, without a thought?

Q: *There is nothing wrong or right.*

Bob: There is nothing you can say without a thought. But, again, you didn't fall apart. You didn't disappear!

Q: *No.*

Bob: There is a beingness, there is something there that you can't even grasp or put a label on. That is why I say you can't conceptualize it or grasp it with the mind.

Q: *Yes.*

Bob: Realize that livingness, that essence, that intelligence-energy or whatever you call it. As soon as I open my mouth I'm using a concept, too! That is why we can only point you towards it. That intrinsic awareness is with you constantly. It is there effortlessly. It is unceasingly arising.

Q: *You are saying that at some point, if I somehow get past this idea of mind and contemplate, that I will have an experience of what is before thought?*

Bob: No. Where do you experience anything? In the mind?

Q: *In the body or the mind, yes.*

Bob: You are the experiencing. You are seeing. Before it is split up into the seer, before it comes into 'I see this', there is seeing happening in the immediacy of now, isn't there?

Q: Yes.

Bob: Then the thought comes up 'I see'. That thought 'I see' is only a thought. But that becomes the pseudo subject: 'I see'. The thing it is seeing becomes the object – for example, 'I see the chair'. So, seeing has been split up into the seer, the subject, and the seen, the object. Actually, the fact of things that is happening right now is just the seeing. That is the same as the awareness or the experience. Experiencing is happening; or the being is happening. It is not split up into the experiencer or the experience. It can be with the mind. But understand that you are the actual functioning itself that is happening in this moment.

17. The Natural State

Bob: They call this the 'natural state'. That is what 'Nisargadatta' means. 'Nisarga' means 'natural'. 'Datta', of course, was Dattatreya, who was supposed to be the primary guru or original guru. Have a look at nature and take your clues from nature. You will see that nature is always functioning in the pairs of opposites. Now, when it is winter, nature doesn't accept one and negate the other. Nor does it reject it. It doesn't say 'I wish it was summertime'. When it is winter, it is winter. Full stop. It'll move on and eventually become summer. When the tide is in it doesn't say 'I wish the tide was out'. It takes its time: four hours coming in; it stays in for four hours; and four hours going out; it stays out for four hours. The opposites are continually functioning in nature. But they are not in opposition. There is no resistance to them. One comes along and the other will take its place. With us, the opposites continually function because we are that natural functioning. We are the same microcosm as the macrocosm. But when the opposites come and we think, 'This one is good; I want more of it', or 'That one is bad; I don't want it', there is constant resistance to them. That resistance is conflict, and that is where we are uneasy. All our anxieties and fears and things come about that way.

If anger is there, well, let it be there! It won't last long. It has got nothing to fixate on. As soon as you label it 'anger', where are you labelling it from? You have had this experience before and you remember what you call 'anger'. So, the same experience, the same feeling, might come up and you label it from the past as anger or fear or whatever. You label from the past, instead of being with it as it is. If you are with it as it is, you might see it as an entirely different emotion that you don't need to label. But the resistance there is hangs around and it builds up. Then comes the condemning yourself afterwards for being that way. It keeps perpetuating itself from that. If it comes up, it will come up and go. The next thing will come up and play around and go.

You can all be sitting there quite seriously, and then someone says something and you all burst into laughter. That comes up as easily and effortlessly as anything. Now, nobody condemns themselves for laughing. But sadness comes up and a tear comes along and we think, 'I shouldn't be like this'. Yet, you can laugh so hard at times that the tears will come. You can be crying laughing. That is OK. But there is a certain aspect of it where you label it and think you shouldn't be like that.

Q: So, Bob, if you find yourself yelling at this seeming person, is that just yelling happening because there is still belief that there is a 'me'?

Bob: If you understand that there is no 'me', you will see.

Q: Because I had an explosion the other night. It didn't last long, and it felt good. But it was just like, if I didn't label it, it was just like energy. A lot of words were said that weren't meant, but ...

Bob: Did you carry it around afterwards?

Q: No. I mean there was little bit of 'Oh, I shouldn't have done that'. But I did. (Laughter)

Bob: A little bit of it out of a habit pattern.

Q: So, it is a habit pattern.

Bob: Did you want to explode?

Q: No. That wasn't the intention.

Bob: It came up.

Q: It just came up.

Bob: Yes. It just shows that you have got no choice.

Q: *Why does that happen when two people get together? Is it just that 'me' coming up against a 'me'? Is it the belief in a 'me' coming up against the belief in a 'me'?*

Bob: While you believe in it, it is. But if you don't believe in it, it is just what is happening.

Q: *Some kind of buttons seem to get pushed.*

Bob: That is part of the functioning, too. That is the way it is happening.

Q: *It is just meant to be happening like that?*

Bob: Yes.

Q: *When you ignore each other? That is just happening too?*

Bob: Do you choose to do it?

Q: *No! I try not to!*

Bob: If you had the choice, you would all want to be Buddhas and perfect, but none of us are. Are there two 'me's'? Have a look now and investigate and see. Is there a 'me' there?

Q: *No. I can't find one.*

Bob: You can't find one. If you can't find one now, and you see it is false now, could you ever have had one? Though you believed there was, was there ever one there? You see from that, that any event that has happened in your life has never been from the point of view of a 'me'. Because there never, ever was one! So, it just shows that that pattern of energy is being lived. All the anger, all the fear, all the love, all the hate, everything just happened. It hasn't been done by a separate entity or the belief in a separate entity or anything.

— 70 —

It is the way it has happened. It is the way that pattern has been lived. It is just the same as it grew you from the time you were a sperm and an ovum. It grew that body, and it is growing it right now. It has been all your thoughts; it has been all your feelings; it has been all your emotions; all the activities in life; your broken bones, if you had them; your healings; your sicknesses; whatever has happened.

Q: Since you have had the understanding for so long now, do you still have moments of anger or explosiveness happen?

Bob: Yes!

Q: It still lives through you and pushes buttons?

Bob: All the emotions are still there.

Q: Oh, great! (Laughter)

Bob: All the thinking is the same way. It will never be any other way.

Q: Of course.

Bob: This is embodied. I can't think in any other way than in the pairs of opposites: good/bad, pleasant/painful, happy/sad. The big difference is there is no reference point which they continually refer to.

Q: You don't feel bad if you do explode or good if you are loving?

Bob: Yes, a bad feeling will come up for while. But it doesn't hang around now as much as it used to, where it would go on for days. As soon as that feeling was there, it kept getting reinforced with 'I shouldn't have done it' or 'This shouldn't have happened'. It doesn't get reinforced. That is what is. It is just what is.

Q: What is the point of looking back at anything?

Bob: Why waste time looking back? It is good to have memory to use at times, but why waste time looking back when you can be totally with what is, right now? You will find the spontaneous, intuitive activity will take place right now.

18. In Essence, It is Now

Q: I have read your book front to back. Now I just open occasionally at wherever I open the page. It is like you said, there are things in there that didn't resonate when I read them the first time. Now it is like, 'Oh! That is what he has been talking about, right'. I read something today about how that 'me' is just a collection of images from the past that is dead. Something about that really became clear. There is nothing you can do to make anything happen. There is nothing you can do to stop anything happening is there? It is just happening as it is happening.

Bob: Yes. If anything needs to be done, it'll happen.

Q: Yes.

Bob: Bankei, a Zen Buddhist monk, says, 'Everything is perfectly resolved in the Unborn'. They called it the Unborn Buddha Mind. Everything is perfectly resolved in that.

Q: The patterns that you had before, no doubt because of the momentum, keep repeating, but there would be no one to identify with them?

Bob: Yes. A lot of them drop away. I never overcame them or I never beat them. They just drop away. Some still hang around.

Q: If they are there, they are there; and if they are not, they are not.

Bob: Nisargadatta says, 'Occasionally the old patterns will appear in the mind'. But, he says, 'They are seen and discarded'.

Q: I'm more and more getting the feeling that existence is benevolent. I'm just getting the feeling that everything is OK, no matter what happens.

Bob: Yes. That underlying feeling, that sense of well-being, that everything is OK, is constantly there, no matter what goes on.

Q: Yes.

Bob: It is hard to explain.

Q: That point that you don't have any reference point, do you have that all the time? Have you no reference points all day?

Bob: No! There might be seeming reference points here. Naturally, there will be seeming preferences, seeming reference points, seeming decisions made, seeming opinions held, seeming choices made. But I know for certain there is no reference point, there is no choice-maker, etc. In your living before there was no centre there, and we did all these things where we thought 'we' did this, chose this, preferred that, liked that and disliked that. There is no 'me' now and there was never any 'me' then. So, they still come up, but there is no belief in a reference point there.

Q: That happens all throughout the day?

Bob: Yes.

Q: Because I know I'm not there yet.

Bob: Have a look at that. You say, 'I'm not there yet'. What does that imply?

Q: It implies there is a reference point.

Bob: It implies time, doesn't it?

Q: *Yes.*

Bob: When were you thinking that?

Q: *Yes, I know that right now I have a reference point.*

Bob: Yes. That was the thought right now. But what was that thought actually?

Q: *It was just a thought.*

Bob: Yes, but when was it happening? Wasn't it happening presently?

Q: *Everything is happening presently.*

Bob: All right. So, what is it? It was presence!

Q: *Yes.*

Bob: In essence it was presence. So, when you say 'I'm not there yet', instead of going into the content, 'I'm not there yet', realize that this is presence. So, where can you go from there?

Q: *You can't! You are always here.*

Bob: Even if you are having that idea that 'I'm not there yet', realize that you are having that idea right in the immediacy of now. So, it can only be the immediacy of now. So, it is bullshit! (*Laughs*) The content is bullshit. It is now! In essence, it is now! As long as you have got that subtle implication of 'I'm not there yet', you are in trouble.

19. No Concepts, No Thoughts

Bob: If there are no concepts, no thoughts, what must be there?

Q: I don't want to intellectualize.

Bob: It is not a matter of intellectualizing! Pause for a second, and drop all thought. Just for a second. What can you say about it?

Q: There is no point.

Bob: You are not doing it. Otherwise, you wouldn't say there is no point. Just see that if there is no thought, even for an instant, there is not a thing I can say about it. Without a concept, I cannot say it is peaceful or not peaceful, angry or fearful, good or bad, anything at all. It is just pure awareness. That is not intellectualizing. That is the activity of knowing, the functioning intelligence that is there with you in all its immediacy. That is with all of us right now. There is no separateness in it. It doesn't start here or there or there. (*Pointing around the room.*) It encompasses all of it.

20. Investigating the Mind

Bob: The nature of the mind, as we pointed out before, is a vibration. Its nature is to divide. It is constantly dividing: good/bad, pleasant/painful, happy/sad, loving/hating. It continues to divide. That is why you will never find the answer in the mind. Whichever way you look with the mind will always be in the mind, because it is continually dividing. See how it divides up the functioning, for instance. It is divided into thoughts, feeling and emotions. Really they are one and the same thing. Consciousness is seemingly divided in subconscious and superconscious. But it is one and the same thing. The so-called different levels are all mind-made, conceptual divisions.

Q: If there is awareness and it is through the mind that awareness feels this through, can't it work in reverse? Can't you use your mind to enter awareness?

Bob: It is not a matter of entering it, because the mind is that. In essence, it is awareness vibrating into a pattern that appears as such-and-such. We take the appearance to be real, rather than seeing that it is that. That is how you say it would work in reverse. You look with the mind, which is the only instrument we have got, and see that thought is nothing but a vibration. But the label we put on things, the word, the concept is not the thing. You can say 'water, water' for the rest of your life, but you can't drink the word. You can say 'fire, fire, fire', but the word doesn't burn your mouth as it comes out. So, we are only labelling, conceptualizing and dividing things with the mind. But, it doesn't get away from that awareness whatsoever. It is that awareness, in essence. But we don't see it.

Things will always appear the same as they have always appeared. The thinking will still happen the way it has always happened in the mind. That is why you don't have to have a state of silence or stillness. When you understand it, which you have done with the mind by investigating, you understand the way thought functions and what the so-called mind is and what it is all happening on. In that understanding, you are not bound by it like you were before.

Q: *Thought, in itself, is not negative?*

Bob: No! The mind is not the enemy. It is a wonderfully creative instrument. Like that art *(pointing to a piece of sculpture)*, like the technology in that TV behind you. All these were ideas in somebody's mind. So, in that respect, it is the functioning intelligence-energy expressing through the mind that creates all these things. But at the other end, being a vibration, it moves into the other end and puts the boundaries upon it: 'After all, I'm only human' and 'I'm not good enough' and 'I can't do this' and 'poor me', 'I'm having a terrible life'. That is where the psychological suffering comes in.

See that the reference point, the 'me', or the self-centre that we are referring to is an invalid reference point, because it is based on past memory, past events and experiences and conditioning. It has no substance or independent nature. That reference point can't stand on its own. When you look and see that there is nothing there with any independent nature, well, the thoughts or whatever comes just go through. You let go what needs to be let go. Not that you do it, but it happens that way. There is nowhere for it to take hold. Before seeing this if somebody called you a nasty name it would hit this image. The image doesn't like being called that, and so the anger, the resentment, the guilt or shame or whatever would come up with it. Now you know what it's referring to is just an image that has no substance or independent nature. It goes right through.

With the investigation, you understand that there is no centre here. So, you must also understand that there is no centre there or anywhere else. So, who can be superior to whom? Or who can be inferior to whom? It is just all part of the functioning.

21. Livingness is Happening

Bob: I have been living this for over twenty-five years now. All sorts of things have happened to me. This hasn't been a smooth sailing. I lost the farm and everything like that. I got broke. I got very sick. All sorts of things happened. But all the way through there was always that underlying sense of well-being. You do the appropriate things when necessary to try and right the situation. But all that mental anguish, where years before, before I had the understanding, I'd have blown my brains out, it just went along and it turned itself around. It is amazing to watch the effortlessness happening.

It turned it around and brought me back down here. I was able to start talking again (I was up on the farm, there weren't that many people coming). From that, people started to come. Even then, when we thought things were going right we had the health food shops and got out of them, that is when the slump came. We had our money invested on first mortgage and the whole lot went! We were left with nothing again. The same thing again. It wasn't a seeming situation that would have got me into all the psychological trauma or dramas. That eventually turned itself around again in amazing ways also.

The livingness happens. It is just the same as it is ageing this body right now. It is happening. From this point of view, I couldn't care less whether it goes tonight or lasts another twenty years. It doesn't make any difference. It is just like the dream is happening. The pains and aches come into it, the aging process, etc. But there is that underlying sense of well-being, that everything is OK. You can only put it negatively: there is nothing wrong. It does not matter if there are seemingly wrong things going on.

Q: Yes. That can be tested with the course of time when one faces life. You have faced it. You have seen that, which I appreciate. But I don't know it very well.

Bob: If you are thinking along those lines, you will never get there. You have got to start with the immediacy of right now and live right now, constantly. Then you will watch it unfold for you. But as soon as you are going into time, which is a mental concept, you will not find the answer in the mind. Because the mind is time.

The ancients say it is omnipresence. And they mean exactly that. That has come from people down through the ages that have gone into this and have had all sorts of experiences and all sorts of dramas and traumas. But they have lived this, written the scriptures about it, and passed it down from one to another. It worked for them. It has worked for me.

I saw Nisargadatta. He told me the only way I can help anyone is to take them beyond the need for further help. A simple sentence like that. He pointed out what I am trying to point out to you. I was able to see it, and I haven't needed help from that day to this. I could have said, 'Oh, yeah, that is all right, but what if this happens or what if that happens…'. He would have said to me, 'Full stop!!'

22. No Acceptance, No Rejection

Q: There is a point in time where something happens and you can just accept it. What is the next step?

Bob: If it is just what is, it means unaltered, unmodified, uncorrected. There is no acceptance, no rejection, no attachment, no detachment. With acceptance, you are taking a stand somewhere. A thought comes up and you say 'I'll accept that'. If you leave that as it is, that means you are not accepting it nor rejecting it. Then some other thought comes up and you say, 'No, I won't. I don't want it'. So, you are not accepting that or you are not rejecting that; you are not attaching to it or detaching from it. You are leaving it all free to flow. In acceptance, if something come up that might not need to be accepted, you might say, 'I'll hang onto this'. You have still got that clinging to acceptance. You are caught in the conflict again.

Q: I have a question about being aware, being present, not being a person. But it seems to have certain taste to it. It is not completely neutral.

Bob: No. No. It is seemingly no thing, but it is fullness.

Q: I always personalize it, whenever I get the chance.

Bob: Yes. There is no sense trying to grasp it with the mind. That is where you are personalizing it. Realize you don't have to do it. The mind is appearing on that. Sit with it as much as you can. You will see there is sort of a subtleness with what appears to be that no thing. There is a sense of well-being there. You can call it an uncaused joy, if you like. It is not the opposite of sadness. It is uncaused. It is is just a natural sense of well-being, of being well. Everything is

OK. It is very, very subtle. Because we are used to the gross sensations out there, that is why we constantly fixate on them. That is what we have been conditioned to do all our life. Stay with the subtleties of this, and you will start to sense what is there. There is an energy that will light up your face, a sort of radiation, if you like.

Q: You say that is something that cannot be touched by a concept of death?

Bob: Have a look, and you will see that life continually lives on life. It can't know death. Integration is happening in that body now. It continually builds cells and everything. When it turns and goes the opposite direction, disintegration starts. This is what you call death. But in the breaking down of that body, there is life or the enzymes, which start to devour it. The maggots or the worms, the microbes and bacteria or whatever come into it till it is broken down. The body is food for all that. It is giving life to millions of them. It is broken down and goes back into the earth. Or if you burn it in the fire, it goes into ash. Out of that comes more life. Grass or weeds or something will grow. Something will come along and eat those. That something will eat that, which ate those. So, life continually lives on life. Different shapes and forms, different patterns, continually manifest in a variety of forms and shapes.

Q: But, these are all concepts.

Bob: Yes, but 'death' is a concept also. What was born was the sense of 'I am', the thought 'I am'. The acquired mind was what was born when we were about two and a half years old. That is what dies. Because, you cannot say there is a time when you were not. You can only go back so far in you mind. Before that acquired mind, you do not remember. So, you can't say you were not. All you can say is, 'I don't remember'. Nor can you say there will be a time when you will not be. You can only imagine or anticipate. So, it is that thought 'I am' and what is added to it is what is born, and that will die. That can die right now, when you see that it is an erroneous belief. You can die to that thought 'I am'. Just come back to the sense of presence that you are., and realize that that is birthless, deathless, timeless, spaceless, bodiless and mindless. But you can't negate it. You can't say, 'I am not'. Even to be able to say 'I am not', the knowing that you are must be there.

Q: Why am I not always fully aware? Sometimes I have the feeling, 'I really have to concentrate or pay attention'.

Bob: You are total awareness, always and ever. Take the reflections in the mirror. It is total mirror. Have the reflections touched it or contaminated it in any way, though they might appear to? The mirror might appear to be full of reflections, but they haven't touched the mirror in any way. It is the same with that awareness. It is the same with the cloud over the sun. The sun is always there in its totality, no matter how thick the cloud is. You can never really say the sun is not there. After a while you know it is there, despite the thickness of the cloud, even though you are not seeing it.

It is trying to grasp it with the mind, with a concept, that keeps you in the trap. Realize you don't have to. Bring it back to its simplicity always. It is nondual; it is one-without-a-second. Stay with it until that understanding is the norm.

Q: Why is it so hard to stay in that awareness?

Bob: Trying to stay in it makes it hard. Try and get out of space! Whichever way you go, there will be more space out there! It is not hard to stay in space. You can't get out of it. Awareness is the same. You have got a concept of what staying in awareness would be like or what it is. But that concept is not it. It is no thing. It is inexpressible, ineffable.

Q: It is so totally boring to stay in that!

Bob: Be with it and see. It is the very life or livingness. There is nothing boring about the subtlety whatsoever. Why it appears to be boring is because it is no thing to the mind. What the mind has been used to since the time it first started to reason is looking 'out there', grasping, grabbing and looking for bigger and better sensations. The greater, the noisier, the louder, or more beautiful the sensation is, the more it gives a lift or a kick, the better it is. That has become our habit pattern. When you come back to the nothingness, the subtleness, which is no thing, it seems very bland and very boring compared to what the mind has been used to. But stay with it for a while and see. There is a lot more in it than what you believe. Get into that blandness or that boringness or nothingness. Sit with it for a while. Don't try to do anything. Just be with it, and see what comes up out of it. See the subtleties, what I call the uncaused joy, the sense of well -being, all this sort of thing.

Q: One time I stayed a month in a cave. I was just bored to death.

Bob: Yes. But, you see, you were totally in the mind then.

23. Reference Points

Q: Last night I had a real fright. I started thinking about reference points. I was thinking about how the earth is moving, the sun is moving, the galaxy is moving, the universe is moving, my cells are moving and the atoms are moving. There was just no reference point anywhere.

Bob: No. Not a valid one at all, is there?

Q: No.

Bob: They are all constantly changing. So, the reference point you have about yourself, that self-image is constantly changing.

Q: Oh, yes!

Bob: You haven't got the same image about yourself as you had when you were a little child. Only a certain amount of events and experiences that had happened were added to the 'I am' thought. That became your self-image. As you go along, you add more and more to it and forget some. It is constantly and ever changing. Everything is evaluated from that reference point. But that is an invalid reference point also because it is never the same. And above all, it has got no independent nature.

Q: Yes.

Bob: What was fearful? Who had the fright?

Q: I just noticed fear there.

Bob: You immediately claimed it.

Q: Yes.

Bob: Would you know it as fear if you hadn't referred it to the past concept or idea? You have had that emotion or feeling previously and labelled it. So, you are evaluating that from a reference point, aren't you?

Q: Yes.

Bob: If it is just what is, as it is in the moment, and it is just cognized, just registered, is it fear? As soon as we label it fear, we fall into the old trap, an image. If the feeling is there, just fresh and new as it is, without labelling it, see what happens. It is not resisted. It is just what is, unaltered, unmodified, uncorrected. The energy is going to move it, like the energy moves the cloud, doesn't it?

Q: Yes.

Bob: It moves the cloud away.

Q: *It didn't move for a while, because I was resisting it. I went to bed with it. But there is no one to resist it anyway, is there?*

Bob: No! The one to resist it is only what we believe to have some power or some nature of its own. It is that mental image we have about ourselves. It hasn't got any independent nature. Is that right?

Q: (Second questioner) *Is that right?* (Laughs)

Bob: Have you seen if for yourself?

Q: *I have seen if for myself. The mind continues to come up. The only difference is now that when I believe I'm a separate individual, or when I feel like a separate individual, which is quite a lot of the time, I don't care so much because it is like, 'So what?'*

Bob: So, you are not believing it to the same extent.

Q: I'm not trying to resolve it, because there is no resolution.

Bob: You understand that while you have got that body, while the livingness is in that body, the mind is going to think in the same way.

Q: Yes!

Bob: All thoughts are not going to drop away. It continues to vibrate and function the same way. But it has been looked at and the false is seen as false. There is no belief in it anymore.

24. Intrinsic Knowing

Q: Would you say, Bob, that this reality, what appears to us as reality, is no more substantial than a dream?

Bob: No! It is not. It is no more substantial. You carry on in the dream, doing all sorts of activities, but where is the dream figure when you wake up? (*Laughs*) If you went to sleep every night and then dreamed, and the dream carried on from where it left off the previous night, would you be able to tell the difference between this and the waking state?

Q: Right!

Bob: Would you?

Q: It will take some convincing. I can acknowledge it. I have no reason to question it, but it'll take some convincing against my experience.

Bob: Don't let anyone else convince you. I would look at it yourself. The conviction must arise within you. And the confidence of that conviction must arise within you.

Q: Yes.

Bob: It is against all you have been conditioned to believe. But when you look, things start to arise. You have got to look for yourself.

Q: Yes, I accept that. I mean against my experience, what has been put forward appears as a possibility, a little more perhaps, probably likely. But experientially, it is fighting against, it is pushing against something that has taken a lifetime to form.

Bob: It has taken a lifetime to form. But, again, when it is heard it resonates within you, the knowingness of it. It 'rings a bell' as we say.

Q: *It does. That is true.*

Bob: It rings a bell. Even the learnings of a lifetime can't stop that bell from ringing, the knowing, the intrinsic knowing, the innate knowing of it. Allow that to keep coming up. That is what brought you to places like this. That has lived all your life for you. It has turned you around.

Q: *Yes!*

Q: (Second questioner) *Bob, can you just talk about time?*

Bob: Time is mind, really. It is thought. Because, is there a past unless you think about it?

Q: *No, there is not!*

Bob: And there is no future unless you think about it.

Q: *That is right.*

Bob: Time is thought. When do you ever think? Only presently. The actual thinking going on is presently, isn't it?

Q: *Yes.*

Bob: When we are thinking about the past, we are thinking about it presently. So, there is no actual past. When you are thinking about the future, you are thinking about it presently. People say, 'I can't stay in the now because I go into the past or I'm imagining into the future'. But you can never move away from presence.

Q: *No, you don't, obviously.*

Bob: You never move away from it. It is always omnipresence. Time is a mental concept, from that aspect.

Q: *Yes. But if I insulted somebody yesterday, and today I think, 'That was a pretty crummy thing to do. I really should apologize ...'*

Bob: Yes, but see what you have done. You are thinking about the past. You are not back in the past, are you?

Q: *Ah, right. Yes, yes.*

Bob: You can't live the past. You can't live the future. You can think about it. But you think about it presently.

Q: *Always, presently. Of course, yes.*

Bob: We waste so much time—we were just talking about time! (*Laughter*) —in the past and in the future. The actuality is always this moment only. If we are in the past or future, we are missing out on the livingness of this moment.

Q: *But it doesn't negate the fact that if you do something wrong to somebody, you may need to put it right.*

Bob: If you need to apologize or do something like that, well, if he is not there or you can't ring him up or do anything about it, drop it until the appropriate time you can. If you can do it, if it does come up to do it, presently, all right. Otherwise, put that aside till you can actually do it, instead of mulling it over, 'Will I, won't I?' and snowballing it till we get ourselves into trouble with it. The actuality, the actual functioning is the hearing, seeing, tasting, touching, smelling. If we are totally in the head, we are missing out on the other sensations, and we are not living fully.

25. See What It Is

Q: *We are always in the now. There is nothing else.*

Bob: Omnipresence. That is what they say. It is pure and total presence. It is omnipotence, or pure and total power. It is omniscience, or total knowing. There is not even a presence or a now.

Q: (Second questioner) *Can I ask a quick question? This sort of struck home, you said we have never done anything. Even before I started coming here, even in the stupidity, I'd never done anything. But now, understanding this, there is less of that stupidity going on. You were implying that that stupidity is going to continue in the future. But it doesn't quite make sense.*

Bob: What do you mean implying that the stupidity is going to continue?

Q: *I have never done anything. But a lot of my stupidity has been because I think I do it. Now that I realize I'm not doing anything, there should be a lot less. Is that right?*

Bob: Yes! If you are not thinking you have done anything, you have taken that blockage away from the functioning from happening. It wasn't 'you' that had that thinking that you were doing something there in the first place. That is the way it was expressing, with the seeming cloud over it, as it does. Otherwise, there wouldn't be this manifestation as it is. Some appearances turn back and understand themselves. Others don't. But it doesn't make any difference, because nothing ever left that pure essence anyway. It only appears to.

Q: (Third questioner) *Bob, I have been sitting here just listening and also trying to see how the mind divides. It is not happening. It is just not happening. The mind is not dividing anything. There is just looking and hearing.*

Bob: When you are really looking at it, it has got no power to do anything.

Q: There is simply listening to what is going on. There are not even any opinions coming up. There is just listening.

Bob: Just hearing.

Q: Hearing, yes. There is no 'for' or 'against' anything.

Q: (Fourth questioner) That is not happening in my mind! (Others agree) When you talk about feelings, my mind is going, 'But, but, but …' What does that mean about things like anger or sadness? Say, somebody I dearly loved keeled over and died. There would be a feeling there.

Bob: Yes, an emotion.

Q: An emotion, which I feel fine about feeling.

Bob: Yes. I'm not saying you won't be feeling them! But you won't be bound by them.

Q: Ah!

Bob: They are still going to function the same way.

Q: The feeling I get bound by is resentment. I can go all day, all week resenting somebody. Lately, I have been doing what you have talked about. I have been thinking, 'OK, it appears that that is what is gong on. It appears that that is what is happening, Was that my mind ….?' I have been examining it.

Bob: Just ask yourself, 'Who is resentful?' Ask yourself.

Q: *Well, me. I am.*

Bob: Naturally! That is the logical answer, me. But then who is 'me'? Have a look for that. You can say, 'That idiot up there says the "me" is only a thought or an image. Now can I find a "me" there?' Go into it yourself with your mind, looking at your mind. See what that thought 'me' is. Has that thought got any substance? Is it independent? Has it got any spot where it is residing?

Q: *Yes. It is one of the emotions that I forget to do that with.*

Q: (Another questioner) *There is a fear that you are letting go of something else or something. I know, what is there to let go of? But there's this fear of what you would be without it.*

Bob: See what you are without it. Have a look and see what is. If what the fellow says is true, that I'm just that pure intelligence-energy, where can I fall to? There is nowhere I can go that I can fall out of it. Is he right or is he wrong? I'm willing to take a chance and see. You find there is nowhere to fall.

26. Start Questioning These Things

Bob: From the time we started to reason that sense of separation came upon us. As soon as the 'I thought' came upon us, so did its opposite: 'not I' or 'other than I'. With that belief arose a belief in something that is separate from 'I'.

That sense of separation first came upon us when we were about two and a half years old. From that time on, we have been conditioned to seek 'out there', to gather, accumulate and add, to try and make that 'I' complete or whole or stronger. Because where there is 'I' and 'not I', there is a sense of separation, insecurity and vulnerability. From that time on, we are insecure and vulnerable. Because of the conditioning, we search out there and continue to gather, accumulate and acquire, to do everything to make us whole or complete. We even create some spiritual thing, a future time when we will be enlightened or realized, not realizing that we are never separate in the first place. We go on like that until we come to a place like this or hear something or pick up something that turns us around and makes us have a look and start questioning that which we have never questioned before.

27. It is All 'That'

Bob: Who has got the questions? What do you remember of it?

Q: *Last time, you were saying that everything is a concept. Just push away all concepts and everything which appears in your consciousness. Even doing this, you are using a concept.*

Bob: Yes. It is not a matter of pushing the concepts away. It is just a matter of understanding that everything is a concept. As a concept, it is not the actual. The word is not the real. The word is never the thing, is it? You can say 'water, water, water' and you can't drink the word. You can say 'fire, fire, fire'. That word doesn't burn your mouth. It is a description of something or a symbol for something, but it is not the thing. All our concepts about ourself and everything else are not the actual thing. They are just a symbol or a translation. It is not a matter of pushing them out or getting rid of them. It is a matter of seeing and understanding that that is what they are.

Q: *Even understanding must be a concept.*

Bob: No. It is just knowing that they are not the real, that they never move away from that nonduality. In essence they are that awareness. That is a concept, too, to say that. But understand that they are awareness or consciousness or whatever concept you like to put on it. They are that one-without-a-second. In knowing that or understanding that, it doesn't have to be thought about or conceptualized.

Q: *But you are saying 'in knowing that'. Knowing or understanding can only occur through a concept.*

Bob: No. You are knowing right now. You are not conceptualizing, in the immediacy of right now. I'm talking about knowing, the pure intelligence. You know that you are. You cannot negate that, can you? You cannot say, 'I am not'. That knowing that you are is there immediately with you. It is always and ever there with you, isn't it?

Q: *But even that 'knowing that I am' seems to have different levels. When you ask me, 'Are you?', of course, at that moment, I am. But otherwise, I'm not so sure. If I don't think about it ...*

Bob: If you don't think about it, you can't say you are not.

Q: *Yes.*

Bob: You know. There is no concept there. That pure knowingness is there, isn't it?

To translate the knowing that you are, you have got to say 'I am'. But you don't go around saying 'I am, I am' all day, do you? You don't have to, because that innate knowingness is constantly with you. That is prior to any concept, isn't it? See that, and understand that. The understanding that you know, you don't have to conceptualize at all. You are hearing. Before you conceptualize by thinking 'I hear the cars going by' or 'I hear this voice', the hearing is happening, isn't it? The seeing is happening in the immediacy of the moment before the mind even comes into it. That is what they talk about when they say 'prior to the mind'. They are not talking about doing away with the mind and seeing what is behind it. Realize that prior to the mind there is always that pure intelligence or knowingness.

Q: *But it always needs something. This prior intelligence always needs something.*

Bob: To be able to translate anything, there has got to be the appearance of things. Everything is appearance only, but it all can be broken down into that space-like awareness, into nothingness. That body appears to be solid, but actually, it is only the elements. Those elements then can be broken down into subatomic particles and into nothingness. So, in essence, it is still that pure intelligence-energy.

Q: Yes.

Bob: Everything, including all your concepts and thinking, is nothing but a vibration of energy, when it is broken down. The concepts are still only that appearing as concepts. The body is still only that, appearing as a body. The carpet is only that, appearing as a carpet. You can't get away from the simplicity of this thing: nonduality. It means that that is all there is. There is only that. Using the metaphor of space-like awareness, the likening it unto space, you see everything as the content of space. All phenomena are the content of space, aren't they? There is nothing you can postulate or think of or imagine outside of space, because if you imagine anything there has got to be space around it. So, the content of space is really nothing but space, because it can all be broken down again into space. Awareness or intelligence-energy or whatever concept we use to point to your reality is only that. It is all that. It even encompasses the space, because there is awareness or a knowingness of space. But we can't define it as any particular thing, because it has got no shape or no form or no dimension whatsoever. It is the same with that essence that you are. It is similar to that. It is the same intelligence-energy that functions the universe, that keeps the stars in orbit.

Q: Why do we always seem to move away from it? It is so hard to stay in that.

Bob: That is exactly it. You seem to move away from it. But if you understand, you can never move away from it, because everything is that. No matter how it appears, it is still only that. Everything is that. Is that right, Robin?

Q: (Second questioner) Yes, Bob, that is right! Good boy! (Laughter)

Bob: Thank you! Can I go to the top of the class? *(Laughter)*

Q: (Third questioner) *It is a key point actually, isn't it, that everything, absolutely everything, is that.*

Bob: Yes.

Q: Even doubts about whether it is that or not!

Bob: Yes. The seeming obscuration or loss of it is still only that. That is the simplicity of this. It is nondual, one-without-a-second. As it says in Dzogchen, 'non-conceptual, self-shining, ever-fresh, presence-awareness, just this and nothing else'. There is nothing other than that.

28. Sit with This 'No Thing'

Q: In this last week, I have been feeling like a vacuum, but I don't sense it within. I mean, I have labelled it, but I don't sense it within the body, per se. I feel that 'fight or flight' syndrome about coming to terms with not changing anything. I feel it has gone into a mourning. Because my brain is saying, 'Accept it as is', but then it says, 'But don't'. It feels it is like the heart and the mind are not in a congruent state. It leaves me very in the void, as if I don't quite know what the truth is anymore.

Bob: Did you ever know what it was?

Q: Once upon a time, the truth to me was God, Jesus and the Holy Spirit. But I have moved beyond all of that.

Bob: What is left?

Q: I now believe that there is just awareness or presence.

Bob: You will never know what truth is because that which is knowing must be truth itself. You can't negate that. You have gone into the vacuum or everything seems void or empty. But then you are trying to define truth in that voidness and emptiness, but you can't get rid of that, can you?

Q: No.

Bob: That has got no concepts or nothing, no labels.

Q: It is like it is depriving me of intimacy. It is as if when you strive for something, you build up a goal or you get that warm fuzzy feeling that you are working towards something. Here, it is like I'm working towards something that really doesn't exist. It is a concept. It is just space.

Bob: Do you have to work towards it?

Q: *No. I am just it.*

Bob: OK. You say you have seemingly lost the sense of intimacy you had before. Why? Because you haven't got a concept. Just stay with this is-ness for a while. Get used to that. Sense the subtleties that are in that. You have got some image about what intimacy is based on past events and experiences, haven't you? It has become a reference point: it should be like this. Sit with this no thing for awhile. It seems to be no thing.

Q: *I can ... yes.*

Bob: But you can't do anything with it.

Q: *No, I can't do anything with it.* (Laughter)

Bob: Instead of continuing to look for something, take time to be with it openly, not accepting or rejecting, not taking a stance. Just what is, is what is.

30. A Question on Purification

Q: Can you briefly explain your teaching?

Bob: What I try to point out is based on what the ancient traditions tell us. In advaita, for instance, which is the Hindu teaching of nonduality, they say it is exactly that: it is nondual, one-without-a-second. Other great traditions also point out the nondual aspect of it. For instance, in the Dzogchen Buddhist teachings, they say it is 'non-conceptual, self-shining, ever-fresh, presence-awareness, just this and nothing else'. Christianity and a lot of the other traditions talk about the supreme or God. They say it is omnipresence, omnipotence, and omniscience: all power, all presence, and all knowing. To me that shows that there is nothing other than that, that everything is, if you like to use the term, God or spirit. I use the term 'intelligence-energy'. It is only that and nothing but that.

Q: A common view in yoga circles about the nondual understanding is that the mind and body must be purified before one is ready to receive this teaching. Otherwise, it will remain on an intellectual level.

Bob: Again, going back to what I just said. It is all the one. The mind and the body are also that one. It just needs to be looked into and seen that they are all the one essence or the one taste. So, there is really nothing needs to be purified. Nothing can be purified, because it is already pure!

Q: Mmm! I have got nothing else to ask then! (Laughter)

30. Who is the Thinker?

Bob: Any questions?

Q: *Thoughts arise. Thoughts have to precede a choice, because if I am making a conscious choice, it is by thinking about this or that. So, those thoughts have arisen.*

Bob: Who is the thinker in that case?

Q: *Who is the thinker?*

Bob: It is this 'ego me', the belief in the 'ego me' that is the cause of the problem. Have a look within yourself and try and find what you call 'me'. Is it that mind? Is it what we take to be the body-mind entity? That is what it appears to be. But investigate it and see. Are you the body?

Q: *No.*

Bob: Do you really see that?

Q: *Not completely, no.*

Bob: There is no spot in the body of which you can say, 'This is what I am. This is where it all starts', is there?

Q: *Every cell has a consciousness....*

Bob: Yes, every cell has that intelligence. Every cell is made up of intelligence.

Q: *Yes.*

Bob: The whole lot you might call the body, but it started

off with a single cell, didn't it? We know that has long since gone. It has been replaced by other cells. We know there are millions or billions of cells dying and being replaced in the body right now. If there is an entity there, which particular cell are you? The overall group of those cells – some of them are patterning and functioning as livers, some are patterning and functioning as kidneys, some are this, some are something else. We call that 'my' body. But whose body?

The other thing was the mind. That is what is calling the body 'my' body, that is the primary thought 'I am'. You are knowing that you are. Am I that thought? We don't go around thinking 'I, I, I' all day to know that we are, do we?

Q: No. Logically, I'm still here, even when I'm not saying 'I am'.

Bob: Yes! You are knowing that you are. That knowing that you are expresses through the mind as the thought 'I'. But you can't say that there is any entity there which you call 'me'. What you believe 'me' to be though, before it is questioned, is that thought 'I am'. To this, you have added to other thoughts, such as 'I am Robert', 'I'm a male', 'I'm so and so years of age', 'I have done this, and I have done that' and 'things have happened here' and 'I feel fearful about this or anxious about that' or 'I'm happy about this' or 'I want more of this' or 'they shouldn't have done this to me'. What have they done it to? 'Me', yes, which is just this pattern of energy, this bundle of cells that has got a memory that didn't like it or doesn't want it or needs to do something else. So, it has got no substance or independent nature. But you must realize the livingness is there. The beingness is there.

Q: OK. Explain 'independent nature'.

Bob: Without consciousness or awareness, without that knowing that you are, can you have thought?

Q: I can dream when I'm not conscious. They are thoughts, aren't they?

Bob: Pardon?

Q: Are dreams thoughts?

Bob: There is a certain movement of consciousness there. There is a stirring there.

Q: There is a subconscious…

Bob: Don't divide it into subconscious and other-consciousness. You will get lost.

Q: There is an awareness.

Bob: If you are in deep sleep, where are you?

Q: I'm not anywhere. Well, I'm just wherever I am.

Bob: There is no mind going on saying, 'Here I am. I'm asleep, I'm asleep'.

Q: No. No.

Bob: There are no choices being made in deep sleep. If that consciousness is gone altogether, you are then what you call 'dead', aren't you?

Q: Yes, most likely. OK. So, even in deep sleep there is some awareness in the sense that, yes, the body is breathing, the heart is pumping, all the functions are still happening. It is just that the mind is …

Bob: The mind is in abeyance or resting. While you are in that deep sleep the body has changed. More cells have taken over. Some cells have died. If there is any disease there, it has progressed or whatever. So, there is no entity there, as such, with any independent nature of which you can say, 'This is what I am'. But that image you have got about yourself (that 'I'm Robert', and this, that and the other, which you formed based on your past events and experiences) is only a mental image. Without that consciousness, it has got no independent nature. Nor has it got any substance. A mental image hasn't got any substance at all. It is like drawing on water.

31. There is Only That

Bob: There is only That. Everything is That. It can only be that one-without-a-second appearing in diverse shapes and forms. Another metaphor they use for it is 'space-like aware-ness', likening it unto space. Have a look at space in the same way. Everything is in space, isn't it? There is nothing you can postulate or think about or conceptualize outside of space. As soon as you do, what is it going to be in? What is it going to manifest or express in? Now that must manifest or express or appear in space! If it appeared on something solid, what would that something solid be in? In space. By the same token, this pure intelligence-energy or awareness, being space-like, contains everything. Everything is ap-pearing in that. There is nothing outside that. The body, the mind and everything else appears in that. It is one-without-a-second. So, that really must be what you are. But you can't grasp that with a thought or with your mind. The mind can't encompass it. The mind being a thing doesn't want to know about no thing.

All our lives, we have been functioning, and how often have we noticed space? If I ask you what is the first thing you see, you would say you see the wall or something like that. Very few people say, 'Oh, the first thing being seen is space'. Yet, it always is. Even when you have got your eyes closed, there is space between your eyeball and the lid! It is the same with that awareness. The very first thing that happens there, if you look closely, is that obviously you start noticing space more and more. So, the other way around: when you believe that it is all taking place in awareness, obviously you start noticing that there is that awareness there, and thoughts, feelings and emotions, everything is appearing on that awareness. You realize also that you can't cut space; you can't grasp space; you can't stir it up; you can't do anything with it. The same applies to this awareness. There is nothing you can do with it. Nothing can touch it. All your hurts, dramas and traumas have never contaminated it or touched it in any way.

Here is a deeper one or a higher one, if there is such a thing. Another term they use is 'cognizing emptiness'. The cognizing is constantly happening. That is the pure intelligence cognizing everything. Everything is registering just as it is. Cognizing emptiness: how would you take that? 'Oh, I'm seeing emptiness. Now I'm starting to notice the emptiness'. Don't you see, what they are saying is that cognizing is emptiness itself? It is the emptiness that is doing the cognizing. It is the emptiness that is the pure intelligence-energy. Realize that. The very first thing you see in here, when you really look at it, is that there is no head there as such. There is just that emptiness. Everything is being seen from that. You look back into that cognizing emptiness and you see there isn't anything that is a seer or a thinker or a choice- maker. It is all emptiness. These things are displaying on it. This body, the sides of the head you can see, the front of the body—all these things are like the reflections in the mirror. The nature of the mirror is to reflect. It is just clear and empty. But it is reflecting whatever comes near it. The things in the mirror don't contaminate or touch the mirror either.

See that and realize that you are the emptiness itself, the no-thing-ness. See that everything appears and disappears in the space-like awareness or emptiness. Emptiness doesn't mean it is a vacuum or a void. It is cognizing. It is the pure intelligence, the same intelligence that functions this universe. Patterns appear and disappear.

32. Question Your Beliefs

Bob: All this is about really is just questioning your beliefs. You understand that all the problems arise from that idea of a separate entity, the sense of separation. The belief in separation is the cause of all our problems. If you want to be free of that suffering and all the rest of that psychological suffering that goes on, just question and have a look and see. The underlying cause is the 'me', and the effects are my unhappiness or fear or anxiety or stress, resentment, self-pity or whatever. If the cause is seen as false, can there be an effect without a cause? It is as simple as that. There can't be an effect without a cause. So, what happens? If the cause is seen through, what must happen to the effects? They must drop away. It doesn't mean to say that the pairs of opposites won't continue to come up. But they are not believed in or fixated on any more, and the energy just moves on. If you look at the whole manifestation, you see it is in dualism. It is based on the pairs of opposites. If there wasn't silence, there couldn't be sound. If there wasn't stillness, there couldn't be movement. If there wasn't day, there couldn't be night. If there wasn't summer, there couldn't be winter or spring or autumn. The whole lot is dualism, vibrating energy, just appearing in different patterns, shapes and forms.

But understanding it, there is not the bondage that was there before. There is not the bondage of the separate entity that is feeling separate and apart, insecure and vulnerable, trying to be secure and less vulnerable, wanting to change, alter, modify and correct what is, which is a conflict and a dissipation of energy. Without that, just like the universe in that dualistic manifestation, it just flows along of its own accord, effortlessly, and changes come about. Well, the same here. Without that conflict we put upon ourselves, it will flow along and changes will come about, as they are doing anyway, because this body has gone from a little child to a young boy, a youth, an adult. Now it is advancing into old age. Soon it will be kaput! That energy is broken down. All by itself. I'm not trying to make it any older. It might be better if I might be able to make it younger! (*Laughter*) But it happens by itself. We don't take notice that this is happening here by itself.

But with our thinking and the belief in that separate entity, that that thinking created, we think we are running the show! That causes us endless problems.

Q: Is that part of that concept of surrender?

Bob: Yes, but that is a trap also. What are you going to surrender? Or 'who' is it that is going to surrender? We can try for years: 'I have got to let go', 'I have got to surrender' and all the rest. But who? It comes back to that again. The cause, the 'who' or the 'me', has no substance or independent nature of itself. It is just an imagined thing based on past events, experiences and conditioning.

Q: It is like grasping it, but doing nothing. Because once you do it, you are setting up divisions.

Bob: The doing still happens, just like the body is growing and aging. Do you choose your thoughts?

Q: I want to!

Bob: Realize that thoughts are continually coming up. Thinking is happening, just the same as seeing, hearing and everything else. When they come up, the habit is, we continually refer them to the 'me' of past memory and past conditioning. If we weren't doing that, we'd probably be acting spontaneously and intuitively, and the flow would go on. If memory needs to be used, refer then to memory for what to do. That way, memory is being used. But when it uses you and you say 'I'm not good enough', 'I can't do this', or 'This is impossible' or 'What will be the results of this?', 'What will they think of me?' and all this crap we put ourselves through, it is self destructive. That is the way the functioning goes, too. At certain points it pulls people out of that and brings them to where they start to look at this sort of thing.

33. Everything is Reflected

Q: So, choices are being made...

Bob: Yes!

Q: But sometimes they are being made based on memory, sometimes on intuition, and sometimes on reason.

Bob: Yes. But if it comes up from memory or intuition or reason, again, was there any deliberate doing of that? Any deliberate doer? Or does it just come up that way?

Q: Wherever it arises from seems to be one level. Then there is another level where I choose to look at the thoughts or memory and make a decision after that.

Bob: Yes, but who was the choice-maker? Or, did that thought come up, and then another thought came up, 'Now I'll look at this'? Then something else might come up, and you say, 'I chose not to do that'. But there wasn't any choice-maker there. One thought finished, another thought started, and another thought came up. We habitually attribute it to 'me' as the doer until it is thoroughly questioned and seen.

Q: (Second questioner) So, we think it is occurring in here (pointing to his head) ? Don't we?

Bob: Yes.

Q: I mean, that is the illusion.

Bob: Yes.

Q: There is a brain there. A neurologist tells us there is a brain.

The mind is different. There is a brain and then there is what we are calling the mind is the past or what you are calling a thought.

Bob: The brain is just like transistors in the radio. That life-force or energy is jumping from one spark to another and forms a pattern, an image or a thought. As you say, you think it occurs in here. But go back to what I told you a little while ago: cognizing emptiness. Realize that you are cognizing right now, everything is being registered. Have a look and see where you are cognizing from. It is empty. It is clear and empty there. Try and take that back. It is clear and empty. There is not even a concept of a brain or anything else, or even a head! Then see that everything is reflected in that emptiness; it is being cognized in that emptiness, like everything is reflected in the mirror. You have been told and conditioned and you believe that everything comes through the brain and all the rest of it. Like Douglas Harding always says: on present evidence, what are you actually seeing? Can you see anything here, except clarity and emptiness? There are no thoughts there. When you look at it closely, there is not even a head there. There are not even two eyes, on present evidence. What you are actually seeing is just space. If you look from that to see whether the thought is coming from a brain, you can't see or grasp any brain as such.

Q: This is the illusion. If you ask most people, they'd say the thinking is going on in here (pointing to his head), *wouldn't they?*

Bob: Yes! Exactly. If you asked most people how many eyes they can see, they'd say, 'I have got two'. But what you are actually seeing? All I can see is an open space here. I don't think you see any different, if you look at it closely. You wouldn't know you had two eyes, if there wasn't a mirror to see yourself or you looked at somebody else. If you were the only one on earth, without a mirror, how many eyes would you say you had?

Q: Yes.

— 112 —

Bob: We don't go on present evidence. We go on what we believe, without questioning.

Q: *But because there is a mirror, then you can see the pattern.*

Bob: Yes. That is good. Good that you can. But you don't have to go on believing in the pattern and all the rest of it. It is good. You invented a mirror so we can see the pattern. Now take it a little bit further and question the pattern. Question everything that you have come to believe without questioning, instead of just stopping there, half baked. It is good that we can get a microscope and see things and understand. We have gone a long way 'out there' in developing things and understanding, but we have never questioned ourselves, which is the most essential thing to do. That is where the freedom from this bondage of self lies. That is the 'peace that passeth all understanding'.

Q: *From that perspective, what is explored 'out there' is, in once sense, irrelevant. The more it is explored, the more it is divided.*

Bob: As many have said, the greatest voyage you can ever take is the voyage of self-discovery. It is understandable why we looked out there. It is because we have been conditioned to look out there. When that sense of separation and vulnerability came within the whole set up, it had us looking 'out there' in order to become complete and whole by adding, accumulating, and gaining, gathering. We believed we were separate and vulnerable, not realizing that we were whole from the start, that we never have been separate. So, it is a futile search, really, though in technology and art and everything like that, it has been a wonderful experience, I guess. But in finding ourselves, and freeing ourselves from all this trouble, it has been useless. Because no matter how much we gather, accumulate and gain, we can never become secure or whole or complete. Because there was never any time when we were not secure, whole and complete.

The cognizing is happening with you right now. There is nobody here who is not seeing or hearing, just as it is.

The thought might come up, 'It is so and so'. Realize that that is being cognized also, before it is altered, modified or corrected. If it is altered, modified or corrected, that is being cognized, also. That pure cognizing or registering, as I like to call it, is happening constantly, always. You don't have to kickstart seeing. You don't have to kickstart hearing. You can close your eyes, but you are still seeing the darkness behind your lids. You can put your hands over your ears, and still be hearing the sounds and things. You can't stop it.

By the same token, you cannot be not aware or unaware. People say,'I wasn't aware' or 'I lost it'. How can you, if it is the base on which everything appears and disappears? It is like the sky. All things are appearing in that space-like sky. When was the sky not? Even with the clouds covering it, is it not there? And does the sky know yesterday or today?

But where do you appear, you that believes you think? Without the sky, which is space, could you appear? So, if in that sky-like space you are appearing in, there is thinking going on in that pattern, where is it coming from? Is it particular to that pattern to the exclusion of everything else or what it appeared in? Don't you think there would be the intelligence that formed it, with that ability to think and all the rest of it? That is not independent or exclusive to that particular pattern.

Q: No. What I take to be happening to me, for example, is just things that are happening. If I don't say to myself or think to myself 'That is happening to me, and I don't like it', if I think it is just happening, and I don't identify with it, then I can't be happy or sad or can't react to it in that way, emotionally. It is just happening. You said 'Life feeds on life'. It comes back to there being not much point to it.

Bob: Yes. But you are not realizing that if there is no 'Robert', as such, as an entity now, there never has been a 'Robert' that has done anything. So, when you are thinking 'This is happening to me', and 'I have got to do this', knowing for certain now that there is no 'me', realize that that living-ness, that intelligence lived you up to this point, with all the

belief in the separate entity. That living will continue without that belief. You will still use the terms 'me', 'I have got
to do this' or 'I'm going to choose this thought' or whatever.
But you will understand that there is no personal entity with
any personal volition there that has ever done anything. It
is the intelligence-energy expressing as that pattern 'Robert',
which is unique in its shape and form and the things that
it does, how it is expressing through that intelligence. But
instead of thinking that the whole intelligence is there in
that minute little pattern, the whole universal intelligence-
energy is behind it. You are the unlimited potential, instead
of a bound creature that is bound by the pairs of opposites:
'Oh, I'm not good enough' or 'I can't do this', and the image
or attitude that 'After all, I'm only human'.

*Q: (Second questioner) If you say, 'What is the point or what is
the purpose?' that is by implication referring to a 'me'. Like, what
is the point to my life? What does that mean to my life? By implication, it is a reference point, isn't it?*

Bob: Yes.

Q: The point to 'whom'?

Bob: When you ask 'What is the point?', who wants to
know?

34. Subtle Trap of the Mind

Q: Bob, one of the questions that I have, and I know it is a concept, is that one can grasp the discussion intellectually, but it is almost like it has to translate into a livingness or something. Do you know what I mean? I know it is quite dividing.

Bob: It is! Because, where do you get the idea 'intellectually' from? Why put on that label? Grasp it. Full stop.

Q: I'm assuming life should just turn upside down or something or shift dramatically or maybe it does. I don't know.

Bob: It may or it may not, but it doesn't need to, does it? You see that there is no 'me'. There has never been a 'me'. Why hasn't life turned upside down before?

Q: It is just a concept.

Bob: Yes. You put the label on it: 'I understand intellectually'. Then we think there is some other way that it needs to be understood. Then we are subtly back in the trap of the mind. Seeing it is seeing it. Two and two is four. Is that intellectual? Or is there a knowing of it? In the seeing of it, nobody can convince you otherwise. The same with this. It needs to be looked at to really see that there is nothing there with any substance or any independent nature that I can call 'me', nothing whatsoever. But thinking is still happening. Seeing is still happening. Hearing is still happening. Feeling, etc. Everything is still happening the way it always has. Choices are made. Preferences are held. Arguments, fights ... livingness goes on.

Q: But it is from a different state of awareness...?

Bob: It is not different. It is all awareness, but the only thing that happens is that psychological suffering drops off, including the resentments, fears, self-pity, depressions and all that sort of thing. The emotions come up, but they don't hang around and fixate. The anxiety does not build up and build up. The knots in the guts, aches in the hearts, lumps in the throat, and feelings that go on in the body because of that are not there.

Q: (Second questioner) *What sometimes comes up is the idea that this is not right. You should be feeling guilty! It is funny how those thoughts continue!*

Bob: Yes. That is the habit pattern, the idea that we have got to conform with what society dictates we should be like.

Q: *It is not attaching to the thoughts.*

Bob: Yes, not fixating on them. Taking what they call a 'vested interest' in it, it hangs around and hangs around. Thought comes up and there is an awareness of it. It will play around for a while and move on. Have a look at your thoughts. Where are yesterday's thoughts now? No thought hangs around forever. It is soon replaced by another thought. Then we say, 'I had the same thought yesterday'. But did you? Is it the same thought? Or did it come up again fresh and new? It might be the same content and the same label on it and all the rest of it, but it is just what has come up right now.

35. The Implication of Two

Q: I know I keep asking this, but, it keeps coming up. You talk about there being such intelligence: the stars, the earth, the cells knowing what to do, etc. Yet, it is the same intelligence that is creating the habit, the thoughts coming up all the time. It is that same intelligence making us feel like we don't get it or haven't got it. It almost sort of implies that there are two things. There is that intelligence, but that intelligence uses you, this pattern, as it feels it wants to and needs to. Or it makes itself believe, the intelligence makes itself believe it is knocking on the door. You knock on the door, you answer. It is the intelligence knocking on the door and answering it at the same time. But yet there either is a separation, there is this pattern and the intelligence using it as it wants to, or there is the intelligence almost like having fun with itself, bringing up habits, bringing up thoughts, bringing up these sort of things, concepts. I mean, if I'm not making concepts then it is pure intelligence-energy creating these thoughts or concepts. Something doesn't quite sit right.

Bob: What is it all? It is all appearance only. Like I say, nothing has ever really happened. Patterns of energy form. There is movement. It is moving this way and that way, forming into different shapes and patterns, which you can call a 'thought' or an 'ignorant thought' or a 'dreadful thought' or whatever. It forms as bodies, minds, stars and everything else, but it has never changed its true nature. In essence, it is still that pure intelligence appearing in different shapes and forms and different patterns. When you dream, is there any rhyme or reason to the dream, as a rule?

Q: No.

Bob: It is like asking yourself, 'Why didn't the dream character understand this, or in the dream, why didn't they see it this way?' When you wake up, the dream is not contained outside of sleep. It was just another appearance or movement in sleep, with no substance or independent nature whatsoever. So, it is one-without-second. Nothing has ever really happened.

Q: *This is, in the analogy of the dream, an appearance in awareness?*

Bob: In essence, it is only awareness, but not in the shape and form. But we believe in the shape and form.

Q: *But we can't believe in it because it wasn't us in the first place.*

Bob: No!

Q: *It was pure intelligence-energy.*

Bob: Yes. The belief in it is another pattern, another shape and form. Now that is appearing. The waking up or questioning of it is another pattern, if that happens. If it doesn't, what is gained and what is lost? It really doesn't matter if there is a waking up or not if you understand that what you are has never been touched! I never can be and never will be.

Q: *Is that why Buddha laughed? When he got enlightened under the bodhi tree, he laughed?*

Bob: Yes. It is all a big joke!

Q: *But it is like you were saying before. I really think that I have grasped that idea that the 'I' that I call 'I' from thought... I can sort of see through that in one sense. I needn't feel through it. But, it is like, once you do that, the world should change. It should be different. In a sense, it actually is, when I have been able to live in that 'do what is in front of me' space, when I have been able to stop worrying about what is going to happen tomorrow and what I did wrong yesterday, and just do what is in front of me. It is different.*

— 119 —

Bob: The important thing is, when you see that, does it have the same substantiality as it did before?

Q: What do you mean?

Bob: Does it seem as concrete and real as we believed it to be when you see that there is no reference point?

Q: No, it doesn't. That is probably part of the problem. Because when it starts to lose that substantiality, you start to worry.

Bob: Once you see it a little bit, you can never go back! Once you question something and see the falseness of it, you can't say 'Stuff this' or 'I'm going back to the old way'. You can't! It has got you! That is why they say 'Your head is in the tiger's mouth'! That is just another way of putting it. You are always that anyway.

Q: It is a huge thing to give up, the concept of 'I'. It is such a huge thing to attempt to give up.

Bob: See the subtlety of that. That would be the 'I' trying to attempt to give it up. It can't happen. All that is necessary is to see that it never had any independent nature or existence of itself. It is only a mental image, a mental picture. Seeing and knowing that, there is no struggle to give it up. It never was!

36. The Mind Translates

Bob: When you realize that you never find an answer to it in the mind, what happens? Without trying to do anything, that sense of looking there sort of drops away. When that drops away, the energy of beliefs is not going into all this thinking. That energy is there to be utilized in the moment. It makes a big difference.

Q: *It is incredibly freeing.*

Bob: Yes. We always thought and believed that we were going to work it out sooner or later in the mind. That constant struggle, that constant dissipation of energy is happening. No matter how hard we look there, we will never find the answer because the mind can't contain it. The mind, being a thing, can't grasp or contain no thing. So, what is the point in looking? Full stop. Like the questioner and the question, when you see that the questioner is the question itself, there is no question and no questioner. Full stop.

Q: *There is a logic that comes in that says that if I don't think about it, then something might happen. It is that fear. I know you say the answers aren't in the mind, but if you think about something long enough, maybe you will arrive at a solution.*

Bob: Well, have you?

Q: *No. (Laughs)*

Bob: How long are you going to think about something until that dawns on you that maybe the answer is not there?

Q: *Yes. But it will be a thought that propels me to move eventually, when I do decide I'm going to go and do something.*

Bob: Yes. But thinking comes up, with a so-called thought, from intelligence, and the movement happens from there. But the movement will happen without the thought also.

Q: Yes. I have seen that.

Bob: All the thought does is translate what is coming from that intelligence, puts it into words. The thought is just the labelling or translating what is happening in that pure intelligence. As I have said before, that so-called thinker or seer or hearer cannot do a thing of itself. The thought 'I see' cannot see. The thought 'I hear' cannot hear. The thought 'I think' is not the thinking.

37. Two Plus Two Equals Four

Bob: When you were a little child, you learned two and two is four, didn't you? You looked at it in every which way and saw that it couldn't possibly be any other thing. Now if somebody said to you that two and two was six, what would you say?

Q: *It could be possible.*

Bob: You think it could be possible? Intelligence would tell you that two and two is four. It can never be six or five. If somebody told you differently you couldn't believe that again because intelligence knows, the knowingness is translated in the mind. When energy or belief has gone into the idea that you are a separate entity, then question that and have a look. You can look for the centre in this body. You can't find one. You can break this body down into elements. You can break it down into sub-atomic particles, into nothing, really.

If you believe you are the mind, have a look at your mind with the mind. You will see that there is no such thing as mind. Show me your mind. There is no thing with any substance of which you can say, 'This is my mind'. All you need to do is see that, apart from thought, there is no such thing as mind. What is thought? You will see that thought is subtle words, at the unspoken level. At the spoken level, it is sounds. Sound is a vibration. Vibration is a movement of energy. So, that is nothing of any substance or independent nature. They are all that oneness, appearing as thought, appearing as the body, appearing as a group of cells in the body, which might be your liver or your heart. It can be broken down in the same way into nothing.

Q: *But we condense it down to this oneness. What does it? What condenses it down to that oneness?*

Bob: Seeing through intelligence. It just requires a bit of reasoning, a bit of looking.

Q: *But it is still thought.*

Bob: It translated as thought. But you know this without thought, as I just showed you before. You are seeing; you are hearing; and the knowingness, the intelligence is there without thought. I'm not saying knowing 'this' or knowing 'that', just pure knowing, the knowing that you are. You can't negate that. You don't need a thought to say that you are. The thought 'I am' has been the translation of that knowing that you are. We have believed that 'I am' to be real, and added to that 'I am' ideas such as 'I'm a good bloke', 'I'm a bad bloke', 'I have got high self-esteem or low-esteem', 'I have done this or done that'. You add all this to the 'I am', and that is what you believe yourself to be.

See what I just said a moment ago. That knowing that you are is there prior to that thought 'I am'. You don't have to go around all day telling yourself 'I am, I am, I am' to know that you are, do you?

Q: *No.*

Bob: If you go back to when you were a little child, before you could reason, before that acquired mind started, that knowing that you are was there. You were aware then, just the same as you are aware now. That is intelligence, not the intellect.

Q: *For me, it is still a thought. It is still the mind that is telling me.*

Bob: Yes. That is why, as I said before, you have got to discriminate between the two and see.

Q: *I don't experience it. But the knower of the awareness is secondary. That is the mind.*

Bob: Yes. But you can't say you are not. You can't say you are not aware, can you? Or can you? If you say, 'I'm not aware', how do you know? There is a knowing of that awareness. There is an awareness. There is a knowing of your not knowing. That is intelligence.

If this mind were running the show, you would be making sure that you took the next breath. Are you thinking about that, taking your next breath?

Q: The mind is telling me my heart is beating, my cells are expanding, etc.

Bob: Yes, it is translating it and telling you that. But do you need to tell yourself that?

Q: I don't have any proof that this body is, except my mind. If I didn't have any senses or even if I close my eyes, I can't even feel if I have toes or horseshoes or whatever.

Bob: Exactly. The mind is an instrument that seemingly gives you the proof. But it has no power or independent nature of itself. Understand that also. It is not independent of that awareness or consciousness.

38. We Take the Label to Be Real

Bob: It is all very well to say 'I don't control it'. That is a sort of copping out in a way. You have got to see. We will take it from the start: 'I am confused'. What happens? You are aware. That sense of presence is constantly with you, isn't it?

Q: Yes.

Bob: How does it express through the mind? The primary thought is 'I am'. That sense of presence expresses itself as that thought 'I am'. The mind can't grasp 'I am' because it is nothing. It is just a couple of letters. To give it some seeming substance, the mind adds the concept 'I am confused'. Now you have got a picture of what that 'I am' is. You see what it has done? It has added a label. Now the mind has got an image it can sort of grasp. It has got this image: 'This is me', 'This confusion, this feeling of confusion, this fear, it is me'. You grasp 'I am' of itself. 'I am' is just that sense of presence. It is a thought. It is that basic thought, though. But we can't do anything with that thought, except add to it events, experiences and conditioning, in order to form a mental picture about yourself. Without adding those events, experiences or conditioning, it is just 'I am'. What is 'I am'? 'Am' is part of the verb 'to be'—'am', 'are', 'is'. And 'I am' is just the knowingness that you are. You don't even have to say 'I am' to know that you are. You can discard that thought even.

Q: Yes.

Bob: You are going around all day not saying 'I am'. You are not even thinking 'I am'. But you can't negate that beingness at any time.

Q: Yes.

Bob: Everything becomes relative to that image you have about yourself: 'I am confused'.

Q: (Second questioner) *The first thing I notice being added to 'I am' is 'I am the body'.*

Bob: Yes. That is another label, too, isn't it? 'Body', where did you get that name from?

Q: *I learned it from society.*

Bob: Yes. You put that label on, and we believe we are this body and the mind. But what is 'body'?

Q: *The elements.*

Bob: The elements. What are the elements? Energy.

Q: *Energy, yes, space.*

Bob: Yes. They are really insubstantial and not independent. So, when we are taking it with the label, we are taking it to be real. You can't find any centre in that body. There is not a particular point where you can say, 'This is where it starts'. And any of those elements, where do they start? Do they start with this body? Is the space inside the body any different from the space outside the body?

Q: *No!*

Bob: Is the air in the body and different from the air outside the body?

Q: *No.*

Bob: Is the water in the body....

Q: No.

Bob: You can't say that they start here in this body. They are universal. You are that. So, you're telling yourself crap when you say, 'I am the body'. You are putting a boundary, a limitation, on the infinite.

39. Seeing

(Sounds of cars and coughing in the room)

Bob: You are hearing the cars go by? You hear that cough? You are seeing the things in the room? What does all that appear on? Wasn't there an awareness of it all? You weren't even labelling a lot of it. Thought with the labelling hadn't come into it. There is just that pure awareness registering everything as it is. Then it is labeled, and we take the label to be the thing.

Thinking is arising also? You are aware of thoughts? Like the cars going by and the things you are seeing, they are all things you are aware of. Thinking is arising.There is an awareness of that also. So, that is not you either. The thought itself is not you. The actual thinking process, the actual functioning, the essence of it is you.

Q: What I want to understand is how that awareness becomes personal.

Bob: It doesn't become personal. Awareness never becomes. It is awareness, awareness, awareness. Full stop. The energy goes into that erroneous belief which has never been questioned, never looked at. It is seemingly personal. If you have a look at a thought or the mind, all thought does is translate what is happening. You are seeing right now, and the thought comes up 'I see'. But realize that you were seeing before the thought 'I see' came up. You are still seeing now, even if you are thinking 'I see'. So, it doesn't change. You are still hearing, as well. You are not thinking, 'I am hearing and seeing'. When it is translated as 'I see', the idea 'I see' seemingly believes itself to be a seer, a subject. What I see, the object, is the seen. Seeing is seemingly divided into 'seer' and 'seen'. But have a look at it. Can there be a seer without seeing? (*pause*) Can there? Can there be the seen without seeing? So, the actuality, the main thing, is the seeing or the hearing or the thinking, without a division.

The thought 'I see' is a thought. The label we put on what is being seen (for example, 'the chair' or the 'table') is a thought also. When the thought 'I see' sees the chair, my next thought might be 'I don't like it'. That is a thought that resists that image of the chair, because it doesn't like it. It is thought resisting thought. That is conflict. When there is conflict, we are not at ease. That is dis-ease. First, there is seeing and registering just as it is, unaltered, unmodified, uncorrected. When the idea that 'I see' or 'I do' or 'I choose' or whatever comes up, there is resistance. That is why we are in conflict.

Q: There is always that sense, that thought 'I'm in this world', especially when you are by yourself.

Bob: Did you ever have a look at it from the other point of view: the world is in me? Because if that knowingness wasn't there, would there be a world? Again, we attribute it to that image we have about it: 'This is my world'. But the world is in that essence. It is appearing in that essence or awareness that I am.

Q: But when I say, 'This is my world', it seems like, somehow, it is not as objective as it is. Because everything is just the way I see the world. I don't think a world exists, except for that subjective experience.

Bob: Does the world disappear when you are asleep?

Q: I think so. (Laughs)

Bob: To the seeming subject, yes. But there is a knowingness that it is there, just the same, isn't there?

Q: It is still there.

Bob: You expect it to be there when you wake up?

Q: But can the world exist outside of that subjective experience of a world?

Bob: The world, really, is appearance only, the same as everything else. It is all appearing on that pure awareness, which is no thing. It has no shape. It has no form. It has no boundaries. It has no dimension. But it is not a vacuum or a void. It is not an emptiness. It is the unlimited potential from which all appearances and possibilities can vibrate into manifestation; all the shapes and forms, from the smallest bacteria to the largest galaxy, even many possibilities that we are not aware of or know of. But they are all appearances. In essence, they've never changed their true nature.

They use the metaphor 'space-like awareness'. Has space got any dimension?

Q: No.

Bob: Everything in space can be broken down into space, can't it? You can take this body and pulverize it into dust, and the wind would come along and blow it away in atoms. If this world were to blow up tonight, there wouldn't be one particle that would be outside of space. You couldn't call it a world then, not in the shape and form it is now. But every atom of it would be there. Nothing would really be lost. It is the same with this body when it dies. Only the seeming sense of this personal entity would be lost, but that is not there to know that even. The personal entity goes along with that. But nothing would be lost, and nothing would be added to it, and nothing would be taken away.

40. Impersonal, Pure Knowing

Bob: 'No thing' cannot be grasped by a thought. That is where we get lost and confused. We think we can get it in our little minds and conceptualize some shape or form. We imagine that 'This is it', this is the great enlightenment or whatever. Or we have some ecstatic experience and think 'This is it'.

Q: *There is only that subjective experience in this no thing. Can there be anything else outside of subjective experience?*

Bob: But is it subjective just to you alone, to that particular point of perception?

Q: *That is a belief, yes.*

Bob: But each one of us in the room is seeing the same world. You see it from a different perspective, but we are all thinking the same way, in the pairs of opposites. But, you are taking the subject as personal. When you see it all as pure subjectivity, there are no objects whatsoever. It is that pure knowing. With the knowing, I don't mean knowing this or knowing that. Without the concepts or the labels, it is just that pure knowing. That is the base of all your experiences, isn't it? If that knowingness wasn't there, how many experiences could you have? That knowingness expresses through those thoughts primarily as the thought 'I am', doesn't it? In the same way, it expresses there as 'I am' and here as 'I am'. It is that same knowingness, which I call pure intelligence, expressing through a different pattern.

41. What Mind is There?

Q: Before the mind, prior to the mind, is it reality?

Bob: You are saying 'prior to the mind'. What mind is there?

Q: The mind of duality.

Bob: What mind is there apart from thought? You are looking in the sense of separation and trying to find the answer. Also, you are looking in time. Before the mind or after the mind implies time. But isn't it omnipresence? It is all right now. The nature of the mind is to divide. That is why I say you will never find the answer in the mind. Because it is doing what it is just doing to you right now: 'Before that, what happened?' or 'After that' or 'Where will I go next?' It will constantly divide and run down some other path. It will keep you going forever and ever. You will never ever find the answer there because some thing cannot grasp no thing. The mind is a thing. It cannot understand, conceptualize or grasp nonduality.

Q: When you say there is vibration of opposites ...

Bob: Have a look. What is vibration? It is a movement, isn't it? It is oscillating back and forth like that, say (*moves his hand back and forth*). It hits a stopper here, which is a label. It hits another stopper there, which is another label: one is good, one is bad, one is pleasant, one is painful. If it is just vibrating as it is, and the appearances are all appearing in it without the labels, what is the problem? In your own actual experiencing you are seeing everything while you are focusing on me and trying to work out what your questions are there. But you are still hearing cars, aren't you? You are still seeing things in the room and hearing other sounds. That is still registering more than what is going on in the mind. In the registering of it, it is not saying 'It is this' or 'It is that' or anything else. Without the thought, it is just what we call just what is. 'What is' means it is there, unaltered, unmodified and uncorrected. So, without the thought, you can't say it is good, bad, pleasant, painful or anything else. But it is still as it is, appearing as it is.

42. Taking Action

Bob: Any questions?

Q: I'm just thinking about taking action. There is always a thought preceding an action. And we have to do things in this world. Do we just come to a place where an action is the right thing to do, without pondering on it? An action is usually into the future. You know, you have got to do something. I'm having difficulty working out how I move forward in my life taking action, without thinking about it.

Bob: Yes. Just have a look and see that the idea of the doer, the entity, is false. Can you see that?

Q: Yes.

Bob: That is only a mental image. It has no substance, because that mental image just dissolves. It has no independent nature. Can you have a mental image if you are not conscious or aware?

Q: No, you can't.

Bob: That is what I mean by saying that it hasn't got any independent nature. It can't stand on its own. That image that you are constantly referring to is nothing, really. It is only an image. Do you see that it is false now?

Q: Mmm.

Bob: When was it ever real? If it is false now, could it have been real at some time?

Q: No.

Bob: That means that there has been no 'Pamela' that has ever lived, ever had any choice or ever done anything of her own personal volition at all. In other words, just like that sperm and ovum came together and grew that body for the first nine months, and then for the next couple of years before the reasoning started. It has grown it. All the actions, all the dramas, all the traumas, everything that has ever happened to you, the idea that you chose something, the idea that you thought something, it has all been done by that functioning intelligence-energy, through that expression you call 'Pamela'. So, you don't need to worry about action. If thoughts will come up about it, then you will think about it beforehand, act on them or not act on them. There is no taking hold of them or fixating on them, no blaming yourself for this or worrying or being concerned about that. That is a dissipation of the energy. Instead, there is just allowing it to function fully in its natural state.

Q: *There is no right or wrong action either, is there?*

Bob: No, no.

Q: *Because really it has no consequence.*

Bob: Do you choose your thoughts?

Q: *No, I don't!* (Laughs)

Bob: Exactly! If you chose your thoughts, why would you ever be unhappy?

Q: *Exactly!*

Bob: There is no choice-maker there. Choices will be made.

Q: *Yes.*

Bob: That means a thought will come up and you will say, 'I'll do this'. The next minute you will say, 'No I won't, I'll do that'. Then you will say, 'Oh, I chose not to do it'.

Q: *Yes.*

Bob: But that thought ceased and another thought came up and took its place.

Q: *Yes. But once again, you are personalizing it and making it into something....*

Bob: Yes, you are personalizing it, and that is the cause of your problem.

Q: *... whereas if you just trust and move forward like a child, you are just in the world and allowing the world to come to you. Then the right action will automatically be appropriate.*

Bob: Yes, but even that 'you' can't allow the world to come to you. Get yourself out of the road all together. It is happening.

Q: *That is true. It is just going to happen.*

Bob: Yes. Life is happening! Have a look again at that essence that you are. With all the dramas and traumas and things that have happened in your life, has that sense of presence been contaminated in anyway by any of those things?

Q: *No, no.*

Bob: The contamination and hurts are only in the mind. They've got to be recalled, presently, to give them any value whatsoever. So, it has never been touched. It has brought you along to where you are right now. It has brought you to look at this sort of stuff. So, do you think it is going to desert you now?

Q: *(Laughs) No!*

43. All 'Time', All 'Places'

Q: It all comes down to there being beliefs which haven't been investigated.

Bob: That is right. Exactly.

Q: (Second questioner) How do you go about investigating them?

Bob: Like we are telling you here all along, you have believed you are the body and the mind. Then have a look. Where is the centre to the body, that you call 'me'? What is the body made up of? That is investigated. It is made up of the elements. What are the elements made up of? They can be broken down into the sub-atomic particles, right down into space, into nothingness. So, that body that is seemingly substantial and seemingly concrete and real is made up of air. You are not separate from the air around you. It is made up of water. You are not separate from the water. You are not separate from the space.

So, your idea or concept of being some substantial entity with some volition of its own gets broken down when you question things along those lines, when you question your beliefs and have a look at it. Understand what the word 'belief' means. Beliefs become a reference point. But belief is not the actual. When you believe something, you have the idea that it could happen or it might happen or it is such as it is. But when you see it and understand it, you are with the actual, not with the belief.

Q: It is the awareness that sees things as they really are.

Bob: Yes.

Q: The awareness sees the beliefs as they really are.

Bob: Yes.

Q: And everything else as well.

Bob: That awareness is registering everything just as it is. What is, again, you know, as is. You are seeing right now. You are not labelling everything you see, but you are still seeing everything without the labels. If there is no label on it, you can't say it is this or that. All it is then is just what it is, appearing as such and such. Intelligence knows what everything is immediately. To be able to express it through the mind, it needs a label.

Q: Yes.

Bob: That sense of presence is expressing through you right now. But to label it, I have got to say 'I am'. 'I am' is the knowing that there is that sense of presence there. That 'I am' thought is taken to be the real. It is taken to be the thing or the essence or the person or the entity that I am. I have added onto the 'I am' the events, experiences and conditioning and formed the mental picture: 'I'm Bob', 'I'm so and so years of age', 'I have done this', 'I have done that'. All this is only a mental image, with seeming substance and independent nature. Everything is referred to that mental image then, because there is the belief that it is something substantial.

But in looking at it, you can break it down and see that it is not substantial, nor is it independent of that awareness. Without that awareness how many thoughts could I have? How many feelings or emotions could I have? That is investigating. You see that; you know that.

Q: Where does the awareness come from?

Bob: Awareness is all there is. You can't say it comes from anywhere, because it is all that there is. We talk about non-

— 139 —

duality. It is never born; it never dies. It is just unceasing. It is constantly and ever and all that there is. Yet, it is no thing that can be grasped in any way, shape or form. It has no beginning and no end, no time, no space. All those things appear in it. They are all things. And things can't grasp what to the thing is no thing. It can't grasp it.

It is just like asking, 'Where does space come from?', when you ask, 'Where does awareness from?' Can you find a centre to space? Can you find a circumference to space? Can you postulate anything outside of space? What would it be in? It must be in space! It is the same with awareness. It is everywhere. It is every 'when'. It is all times and all places.

44. No 'Before' or 'After'

Bob: It is not a matter of us knowing 'this' or 'that' happens. It is a matter of just knowing. That is your basic essence. You cannot negate that knowingness, which is without the 'this' or 'that'. That is pure, space-like awareness. It is that knowingness, that pure intelligence. Do you need any theory for that, that knowingness?

Q: *There is no theory that is going to cover it because it is the endless question. If there were God or the divine intelligence, the question is: 'What was before that?' 'What was before the big bang?' It is hard to say. What was before divine intelligence? Well, nothing. There isn't a theory that will...*

Bob: But all those things—what was before, what was before—imply time, which is mind stuff. We are told that it is timeless, omnipresence.

Q: *What was before timelessness?* (Laughter) *It is the impossible question.*

Bob: There is no 'before' or 'after' in timelessness.

Q: *But the point you have to start from, you have to accept what this intelligence or whatever it is...*

Bob: The point to start from is the fact of your own being.

Q: *Yes.*

Bob: Under any circumstances, can you say 'I am not'?

Q: *I don't think so.*

Bob: Just see that for certain. Start from there. Don't go away from there: the knowing that you are. That is all that is necessary. The rest takes care of itself. But the thing is to focus more on that knowing that you are, instead of the content that is going on. Let the content – that is, the thoughts, the feelings, the emotions, the activities and everything – unfold of its own. This is what is happening anyway, because there is no individual entity that is doing anything.

Q: *There is no individual entity that is doing anything?*

Bob: No.

Q: *It is just happening.*

Q: (Second questioner) *Something that Bob told me that really helped me was when you look without labelling, there is no separation at all. If you just suspend thought for a moment, you are aware of everything, sounds … and just … no separation!*

Bob: See for yourself. You are aware of things on the other side of the room now, aren't you?

Q: *Yes.*

Bob: Is there an awareness up there and an awareness down there? Or does awareness take in what is up there, right from where you are?

Q: (First questioner) *It is just everything I'm aware of.*

Bob: Yes, and you can be aware of the farthest galaxy twenty million light years away, right in this instant, without visualizing it or picturing it. There is just the knowing.

Q: *I can imagine it in me.*

Bob: No, even without imagination. Realize that that awareness can stretch to wherever you like.

Q: Yes. I don't have a problem with time and space in that sense.

Q: (Second questioner) It is like you don't know where to locate yourself. You could be anywhere. There is no centre. There is just looking. I'm as much over there as I am here.

Bob: The 'over there' and 'here' have got to be judged from some reference point, haven't they? With no reference point, can you say it is 'over there'? Can you say it is 'here'?

Q: No!

Bob: We have got to bring the mind or thought into it again to do that.

Q: Yes. That is right.

Bob: Can you say there is an 'inner' or an 'outer'?

Q: There is just awareness and objects.

Bob: Yes.

Q: ... including labels.

Bob: Exactly. Have a look at the sky. Can you show me yesterday's sky?

Q: No!

Bob: ... or tomorrow's sky?

Q: (First questioner) Awareness is not thought?

Bob: No.

Q: How can you have a thought if you don't label something?

Bob: Pardon?

Q: *What are thoughts other than labels?*

Bob: Yes, that is all the thoughts are, just labels. If you are not labelling, you are just seeing straight out, as is.

Q: *Being aware.*

Bob: Yes. I show you this every time you come here. Swing your head over to the right quickly. Back again. What did you see?

Q: *Well, a whole lot of stuff in the corner.*

Bob: Yes. How much did you label?

Q: *Curtain.*

Bob: Curtain?

Q: *A few bits and pieces, but not much.*

Bob: Did you label them?

Q: *A few bits.*

Bob: A few bits. You saw everything, but there was only a certain amount labeled, right?

Q: *Yes.*

Bob: That means that the intelligence is registering every-thing as it is, without the label. Look again without labelling and realize that you are seeing as well as hearing at the same time: my words and that heater going or whatever is going. Realize it is all being registered. The labelling is being registered also. That is a direct introduction to your own natural awareness that is registering everything just as it is. That is the pure intelligence that is cognizing every-thing. When you put the label on it, it is re-cognized. From that, you can understand that that energy is an intelligence. It is a knowing.

Q: *But you can't be aware of a thought unless you label something.*

Bob: Yes, you can. You are aware of thinking, aren't you, if thinking is happening?

Q: *Yes, but all my thinking is happening either in words or images, which are all things.*

Bob: Yes, but realize that before words and images came on there was a registering of them. They are being translated in words and images, as 'such and such'.

Q: *Yes, but how can I realize that without labelling it?*

Bob: There is an innate knowing.

Q: *There is an awareness, but the awareness really only becomes aware when I give it structure, labels or reference points or whatever. If that is not there, you just have this awareness of oneness.*

Bob: Yes. Don't you realize that there is never a time when it is not there?

Q: *No, the awareness is always there.*

Bob: All right.

Q: *I'm happy with that, but how can I be aware of anything? How can 'I'...?*

Bob: You can't be, as that entity.

Q: *Yes.*

Bob: But awareness is just awareness. Like, can the eye see itself?

Q: No.

Bob: You are seeing everything through the eye. But the eye can't see the eye.

Q: No.

Bob: It is the same thing with awareness. Awareness is aware of everything, but it can't know itself as awareness.

Q: Yes.

Bob: It has got no substance or no place where it can sit. We are looking for some ecstatic flash or big bang. But it has been with you constantly all the time and seemingly ignored. It is no thing that can be grasped. It is just this everyday, common place knowing that you are that is with you right now. Some call it 'ordinary awareness'.

About the Publisher

Non-Duality Press publish book and audio resources on the theme of non-duality and *Advaita* with particular emphasis on works by contemporary speakers and authors.

For an up to date catalogue of books and CD's with online ordering visit: www.non-dualitybooks.com

A boxed set of the three CD's of Bob Adamson's talks that form the basis of this book are available to purchase from the publisher.

Printed in the United States
49201LVS00003B/85-111